MURDER
IN AMERICA

Malcolm and Louise Holmes,
my parents (RMH),
my grandparents (STH).
We miss them.

MURDER
IN AMERICA

RONALD M. HOLMES
STEPHEN T. HOLMES

SAGE Publications
International Educational and Professional Publisher
Thousand Oaks   London   New Delhi

For information address:

SAGE Publications, Inc.
2455 Teller Road
Thousand Oaks, California 91320

SAGE Publications Ltd.
6 Bonhill Street
London EC2A 4PU
United Kingdom

SAGE Publications India Pvt. Ltd.
M-32 Market
Greater Kailash I
New Delhi 110 048 India

Printed in the United States of America

Library of Congress Cataloging-in-Publication Data

Holmes, Ronald M.
  Murder in America / Ronald M. Holmes, Stephen T. Holmes.
    p.   cm.
  Includes bibliographical references and index.
  ISBN 0-8039-5054-3 (cl).—ISBN 0-8039-5055-1 (pb)
  1. Murder—United States.   2. Homicide—United States.
I. Holmes, Stephen T.   II. Title.
HV6529.H644 1994
364.1'523'0973—dc20   93-11775
                                                          CIP

94 95 96 97   10 9 8 7 6 5 4 3 2 1

Sage Production Editor: Judith L. Hunter

Contents

Preface

A day does not pass when a murder is not reported. Obviously, the more bizarre the murder, the more attention the media devote to it. For example, when the Jeffrey Dahmer case first came to the attention of the public, we, as experts on serial murder, were besieged by requests for television appearances, radio talk show engagements, and interviews, from California to Florida to Maine. For a day or two we were hot property. Murder sells. However, in teaching a university class titled "The Sociology of Murder" we were somewhat surprised that we could not find an adequate text addressing the various forms of murder that we discussed in class. To this end we decided to write a text that would suit our purposes and that would be useful, informative, and suitable for various classes at other colleges and universities.

There may be some who would debate the types of homicide discussed, or not discussed, in this book. We have chosen to include the types of murder with which we have become most acquainted in our professional capacities as academicians and authors and, in the case of the first author, as a deputy coroner. We have had the opportunity to offer assistance to police departments throughout the United States on more than 300 murder and rape cases. Most of these cases involved sexually motivated homicide, occult-related and ritualistic crimes, mass murder, and murder within families. Our choices also reflect the interests of our students, who over the years have indicated their desire for information about these forms of homicide. We believe the types selected deserve special attention and consideration because they are not adequately covered in existing professional and academic publications. Thus we include chapters that deal with atypical and relatively bizarre homicide, such as serial murder, mass murder, and terrorism and assassination. Other more common types of murder also are discussed: murder committed by children, murder of children, partner homicide, and murder by hate groups such as the Ku Klux Klan. The volume is divided into nine chapters that can be read in any order; each chapter is designed to stand alone.

Although we mention theories in passing throughout this book, our focus is on the pragmatic examination of selected forms of homicide. Trends, methods, motives, statistics, and other descriptive information are dealt with in each chapter. Interested students are encouraged to seek out relevant theories in primary sources that offer more detailed discussion than we can include here. In addition to the numerous journal articles listed in our references, there are many books available, such as Lilly, Cullen, and Ball's (1989) *Criminological Theory: Context and Consequences,* that are valuable resources for serious students who are interested in pursuing further study of the forms of homicide included in this book.

Of course, no work of this type can be completed without the cooperation and understanding of a large number of people. Despite the obvious danger of forgetting someone when listing important contributors, we are willing to run that risk to thank the following people: Chief Douglas Hamilton, Louisville (Kentucky) Police Department; Sergeant David Rivers, Metro-Dade (Florida) Police Department; Detective Jay Whitt, Greensboro (North Carolina) Police Department; Robert Crouse, associate director, Southern Police Institute, University of Louisville; Dr. Richard Greathouse, coroner, Louisville, Kentucky; Dr. George Nichols, medical examiner, State of Kentucky; Dr. Eric Hickey, University of California at Fresno; Dr. Al Carlisle, psychologist at Utah State Prison; Captain Ralph Hernandez, Broward County (Florida) Sheriff's Office; Dr. George Rush, California State University at Long Beach; Dr. Ed Latessa, University of Cincinnati; Jim Massie, parole officer, State of Kentucky; and Chief Jerry Beavers, Asheville (North Carolina) Police Department.

We also owe a great debt to our students. Their interest and questions, demands, and quizzical expressions keep us on our toes. They also keep us mentally alert and eager for the next class.

Finally, our families—especially our wives—deserve special attention. They are attentive to our interests although they do not completely understand our enthusiasm for interviewing serial killers, attending autopsies, or visiting homicide scenes. It might be easier for them if our interests were different. Our wives are sometimes reluctant to answer telephones; they have on more than one occasion answered when serial killers have called from prison, wanting to share some thoughts. To Tootie and Amy go our special thanks.

—Ronald M. Holmes
Stephen T. Holmes

1

Murder in North America

Murder captivates the interest of people all over the world, and no less here in North America. This interest is reflected not only in our reading habits but in popular television programs and Hollywood movies. In the recent film *The Silence of the Lambs,* the main character tries to track down a serial murderer by getting inside the mind of convicted killer Hannibal Lecter; this movie became a national hit. The Rambo and Terminator characters and others in "action" movies further reflect our interest in the world of the violent.

The true character of murder in North America is different from what is depicted in the media—in, for instance, Dirty Harry movies, movies about organized crime figures, and even the "reality programming" genre. In university classes on the sociology of murder, students are visibly shaken when actual murder scenes are shown and cases discussed. When a teleconference call is made from the class to a prison for an interview with an incarcerated serial killer, the students expect to hear a snarling, rabid murderer. Unexpectedly, he is soft-spoken and articulate—not at all what was expected. Scarcely, however, is murder what is expected.

Murder by children, homicide within the family, serial murder, mass murder, and other forms of murder are discussed in the chapters of this book. Undoubtedly, these types of homicide are reflective of our changing society as well as of the changing values and attitudes within society. These changing norms, values, attitudes, and customs are examined here as they relate to acts of homicide.

MURDER: DEFINITIONS

Homicide and *murder* are synonyms. Lunde (1977) defines *murder* as the unlawful killing of a human being with malice aforethought (p. 3). The U.S. Department of Justice's Bureau of Justice Statistics (BJS) (1989) defines *homicide* as the causing the death of another person without legal justification or excuse, and includes the FBI's *Uniform Crime Reports* crimes of murder, nonnegligent manslaughter, and negligent manslaughter (Jamieson & Flanagan, 1988, p. 2). Rush (1991) defines *homicide* simply as "any wilful killing" (p. 147). Thus the terms *homicide* and *murder* are used interchangeably.

Many acts of homicide take place during the commission of other crimes. This distinction becomes important when one considers the two major types of murder. The first type is motivated by instrumental gain. Such murders are part of well-planned activities intended to result in the perpetrators' acquisition of power or property, such as business interests, money, or status. A second type of murder may be called impulsive homicide; it results from sudden action, such as a barroom brawl or other sudden confrontation. In the analysis of these two types of homicides, the location of motivation is the starting point for a discussion and analysis of homicide itself.

LEGAL DEGREES OF MURDER

Typically found in legal discussions of murder is a differentiation between murder in the first degree and murder in the second degree. First-degree murder has two major components: premeditation and deliberation. To qualify as murder in the first degree, a homicide must be considered beforehand. The prosecution in a murder case attempting to establish first-degree murder must prove to the jury that the act was not spontaneous—that the accused considered the act before carrying it out. The second element is that of deliberation. This means that the act of murder was planned—even if only momentarily—and that the act itself was not impulsive.

Murder in the second degree contains an element of malice aforethought but no premeditation or deliberation. The type of malice is also considered in this definition. There are two types of malice, expressed and implied. Expressed malice exists when someone murders another in the absence of any apparent provocation. Implied malice is taken to exist when murder results from negligent or unthinking behavior on the part of the perpetrator.

MANSLAUGHTER

Manslaughter is the unlawful taking of a life without malice or the intent to do harm. Voluntary manslaughter results when there is a death but no malice, although the act is voluntary and the intent is to kill. The lack of malice is what separates this from a case of murder. An example of voluntary manslaughter is a killing committed in the heat of passion, with no planning and no deliberation.

Involuntary manslaughter is the killing of another through some type of negligent behavior. An example is the drunken driver who causes an accident in which another person is killed.

JUSTIFIABLE AND EXCUSABLE HOMICIDE

Another element in the consideration of homicide is whether the act is legally considered justified—for instance, whether it was committed in self-defense or when otherwise permitted by law (see Table 1.1 for a state-by-state list of allowable circumstances under which citizens may use deadly force in defending themselves or their property). In such cases, the resulting death must be considered unavoidable. When confronted by an armed robber, for instance, an individual is generally considered justified in defending him- or herself with whatever amount of physical force is necessary.

TABLE 1.1

State Legal Standards Defining Circumstances Under Which Citizens May Use Deadly Force

State	Even if life is not threatened, deadly force may be justified to protect		Specific Crime
	Dwelling	*Property*	
Alabama	yes	no	arson, burglary, rape, kidnapping, robbery in any degree
Alaska	yes	no	actual commission of a felony
Arizona	yes	no	arson, burglary, kidnapping, aggravated assault
Arkansas	yes	no	felonies as described by statute
California	yes	no	unlawful or forcible entry
Colorado	yes	no	felonies, including assault, robbery, rape, arson, kidnapping
Connecticut	yes	no	any violent crime
Delaware	yes	no	felonious activity
District of Columbia	yes	no	felony
Florida	yes	no	forcible felony
Georgia	yes	yes	actual commission of a forcible felony
Hawaii	yes	yes	felonious property damage, burglary, robbery, etc.
Idaho	yes	yes	felonious breaking and entering
Illinois	yes	yes	forcible felony
Indiana	yes	no	unlawful entry
Iowa	yes	yes	breaking and entering
Kansas	yes	no	breaking and entering, including attempts
Kentucky	no	no	—[a]
Louisiana	yes	no	unlawful entry, including attempts
Maine	yes	no	criminal trespass, kidnapping, rape, arson
Maryland	no	no	—[a]
Massachusetts	no	no	—[a]
Michigan	yes	no	circumstances on a case-by-case basis
Minnesota	yes	no	felony
Mississippi	yes	—[a]	felony, including attempts
Missouri	no	no	—[a]
Montana	yes	yes	any forcible felony
Nebraska	yes	no	unlawful entry, kidnapping, rape
Nevada	yes	—[a]	actual commission of felony
New Hampshire	yes	—[a]	felony
New Jersey	yes	no	burglary, arson, robbery
New Mexico	yes	yes	any felony

continued

TABLE 1.1
Continued

State	Even if life is not threatened, deadly force may be justified to protect		Specific Crime
	Dwelling	Property	
New York	yes	no	burglary, arson, kidnapping, robbery, including attempts
North Carolina	yes	no	intending to commit a felony
North Dakota	yes	no	any violent felony
Ohio	—[a]	—[a]	—[a]
Oklahoma	yes	no	felony within a dwelling
Oregon	yes	—[a]	burglary in a dwelling, including attempts
Pennsylvania	yes	—[a]	burglary or criminal trespass
Rhode Island	yes	—[a]	breaking and entering
South Carolina	no	no	—[a]
South Dakota	yes	—[a]	burglary, including attempts
Tennessee	yes	—[a]	felony
Texas	yes	no	burglary, robbery, theft during the night
Utah	yes	—[a]	felony
Vermont	yes	—[a]	forcible felony
Virginia	no	no	—[a]
Washington	no	no	—[a]
West Virginia	yes	no	any felony
Wisconsin	no	no	—[a]
Wyoming	no	no	—[a]

SOURCE: U.S. Department of Justice, Bureau of Justice Statistics (1989, p. 31).
a. Not specified in the statute.

Excusable homicide is the unintentional killing of another human being. There is no malice aforethought and no negligence involved in the act itself, and the person must be found to have acted in a prudent and reasonable manner, as any other person in a similar situation may have acted.

In the discussion of any type of homicide, the elements of justifiable or excusable behavior, manslaughter, and degrees of homicide are always of interest, and we felt it important to introduce the issue briefly here. However, the scope of this book is limited to an overview of some particular types of homicide committed in North America, and our discussion will not be concerned with such issues for the most part.

Chances of Being a Murder Victim

In 1960   1 in 19,646
In 1990   1 in 10,504

SOURCE: U.S. Senate Judiciary Committee (1991).

HOMICIDE STATISTICS

The Bureau of Justice Statistics (1991a, p. 4, Table 1) has reported that from 1987 to 1991 the number of violent crimes nationwide had increased by 11.7%. The number of murders and nonnegligent homicides had risen by 12.2% (U.S. Department of Justice, BJS, 1991b). In 1991 the Bureau of Justice Statistics reported 6.4 million crimes of violence (U.S. Department of Justice, BJS, 1991a, p. 16) and 12.5 million property crimes (p. 5). The previous high for violent crimes was 6.582 million in 1981 (p. 4). In 1991, there were 173,000 reported rapes, a 33% increase over the previous year (p. 5). Aggravated assault was up also by 6.5%.

Homicide rates can fluctuate severely. Historically, murder rates have differed, sometimes drastically, according to certain selected social core variables, such as age, race, sex, time, and social changes. These differing rates have important implications for academics and practitioners. Academic researchers and theoreticians have for years sought to understand these differences. Practitioners in law enforcement and the judicial system also are concerned with these fluctuations for practical reasons. They must deal with issues of human resources allocation, utilization of other resources, recruitment, policy implications, and public relations. However, thus far the research on homicide and the statistics that research has provided have not been very useful for policy making, because too often they are misleading, unclear, or contradictory. The data are often contaminated by outside situations that interfere with objective data gathering and analysis. Policy makers may be distrustful not only of the results of research, but of researchers themselves. Turf issues, political considerations, and personal biases all can interfere with the setting of strategies to combat this social problem.

Lifetime Risk of Being a Homicide Victim, by Race and Sex	
Black male	1 in 30
Black female	1 in 132
White male	1 in 179
White female	1 in 495

SOURCE: U.S. Department of Justice, BJS (1989, p. 28).

VICTIMS OF HOMICIDE

An individual's risk of being a murder victim appears to depend on certain sociodemographic variables. Sex and race are particularly important. According to the *Sourcebook of Criminal Justice Statistics* (U.S. Department of Justice, BJS, 1991b, p. 403), for example, 78% of murder victims are male, 48.5% are white, and 48.6% are black. The Bureau of Justice Statistics also reports that race and sex are important elements in the likelihood of a person's being a victim of homicide (Jamieson & Flanagan, 1988). As of 1988, the lifetime risk of being a victim of homicide was 1 in 30 for a black male, 1 in 132 for a black female, 1 in 179 for a white male, and 1 in 495 for a white female. Clearly, black males and females are at much greater risk than are whites of either sex. Also as of 1988, in the United States, murder was the eleventh most common way of dying; it was the fourth leading cause of death for children under 14 years of age, second for those between ages 15 and 34, and then became less common as a cause of death as age increased (Jamieson & Flanagan, 1988, p. 28).

The common perception of homicide as a stranger-perpetrated crime does not appear to be accurate. In most cases, murder occurs between people who know each other. In almost 78% of cases, homicides occur between persons who are relatives or personal acquaintances (U.S. Department of Justice, BJS, 1991b, p. 399, Table 3.140). Personal relationships sometimes exist in an atmosphere of hatred, and violence can be the result. Chapter 2, which addresses violence between spousal partners, discusses such violence in more depth.

Characteristics of Homicide Victims

Percentages
Sex
   male   78
   female   22
Age
   under 1   1
   1-14   4
   15-24   29
   25-34   31
   35-44   17
   45-54   7
   55-64   4
   65 and older   7
Race
   white   49
   black   49
   other   1.7
   unknown   .3

SOURCE: U.S. Department of Justice, BJS (1991b, p. 403).

Also included in many persons' ideas about murders is that
most take place during the commission of other felonies. This
does not appear to be the case. According to national statistics
on homicide, only approximately one in five cases of murder
occurs during the commission of another felony or a suspected
felony. Robberies account for the major component within this
category. Sex offenses, which include rape, account for only 2%
of murder cases (U.S. Department of Justice, BJS, 1989, pp. 23-
29). It should be noted that our understanding of the circumstances surrounding murder may be clouded by the fact that the
events leading to a large number of homicides are either unknown or classified simply as "other" or "unknown" (41%).

CHARACTERISTICS OF KILLERS

The research literature on characteristics of those who murder yields a profile of offenders that indicates many have histo-

Percentages of Murders Resulting From Various Situations	
Arguments	39
Felonies	18
robberies	9
narcotics offenses	3
sex offenses	2
arson	1
other	3
Suspected felonies	2
Other	18
Unknown	23

SOURCE: U.S. Department of Justice, BJS (1989, p. 28).

ries of committing personal violence in childhood, against other children, siblings, and small animals. As both children and adults, they tend to be able to maintain only superficial relationships with others. Many male serial murderers, for example, have trouble relating to the opposite sex as adolescents, and feelings of guilt about their sexuality lead them to view women as seductive and tempting creatures (Holmes, 1989; Holmes & De Burger, 1985). Most men who kill are young. Data suggest that most are between the ages of 20 and 40, with the majority closer to 20 (U.S. Department of Justice, BJS, 1991b, p. 404, Table 3.147).

Most killers are male. Many women who kill do so in response to male violence; as Chapter 2 shows, the numbers of women resorting to fatal violence in cases of wife battering appear to be increasing. However, more women also are killing for the same reasons that men have historically murdered. Approximately 12% of murders are now committed by women (U.S. Department of Justice, BJS, 1991b, p. 404, Table 3.147).

Blacks are overrepresented among convicted killers. Statistically, a black male is more likely to kill than is a white male. A black female is also more likely to kill than is a white female. It also must be remembered that most killers murder within their race (U.S. Department of Justice, BJS, 1991b, p. 403, Table

3.146). As noted above, an individual's risk of being a homicide victim is greatly influenced by his or her race and sex.

Homicide rates fluctuate also depending on days of the week and months of the year. For example, most killings occur on weekends. This is not surprising, given the increased numbers of social gatherings, greater intake of alcohol, and other ele- ments of interpersonal interaction that traditionally take place on weekends. Such interaction may lead to increased personal conflicts, and thus to increased violence.

REGIONAL DIFFERENCES IN MURDER RATES

Homicide rates also differ by geographic region (see Table 1.2). The South accounts for slightly more than 40% of all murders in the United States. Gastil (1971) found a relationship between murder rates and residence in the South, as well as increased rates of homicide in states that have particularly great in-migration of residents from southern states. He notes that the following elements contribute to this finding: a southern "fron- tier" mentality, a vengeance mentality, and the availability of firearms. Not everyone agrees with Gastil's conclusions. Er- langer (1976), Lofton and Hill (1974), and others assert that Gastil's claims have not been empirically proven and that the reasons for the high rate of homicide throughout the United States need further study.

According to a report of the U.S. Senate Judiciary Committee (1991), in 1991 the states with the biggest increases were not in the South. New Hampshire, for example, reported only 21 killings in 1990; the number rose to 40 in 1991, an increase of 90%. This dramatic increase is followed by Kansas, an increase of 48%, and Colorado, 40%. North Dakota has an increase of 60%, but the actual numbers are small: 5 killings in 1990 and 8 killings in 1991.

Homicide rates differ not only by region of the country, but by city, county, and state as well. Dallas's murder rate was up more than 30% in 1990; in that same year, murders were up by 60% in nearby Fort Worth (Squiteri, 1991). In New York City, 17 people were murdered in one 24-hour period in July 1991.

TABLE 1.2

Homicides by State, Rate of Change 1990-1991

State	1990	1991	% Change
Alabama	467	410	−11
Alaska	41	50	20
Arizona	284	340	19
Arkansas	241	230	−3
California	3,553	3,550	0
Colorado	138	195	40
Connecticut	166	170	0
Delaware	33	22	−33
District of Columbia	472	475	1
Florida	1,379	1,140	−18
Georgia	76	735	−4
Hawaii	44	12	−73
Idaho	27	23	−15
Illinois	1,182	1,250	6
Indiana	344	370	8
Iowa	54	62	15
Kansas	98	145	48
Kentucky	264	260	0
Louisiana	724	760	4
Maine	30	30	0
Maryland	552	580	6
Massachusetts	243	200	−19
Michigan	971	850	−13
Minnesota	117	100	−13
Mississippi	313	360	16
Missouri	449	500	13
Montana	39	20	−49
Nebraska	43	43	0
Nevada	116	110	−2
New Hampshire	21	40	90
New Jersey	432	350	−19
New Mexico	139	160	15
New York	2,605	2,580	−1
North Carolina	711	730	3
North Dakota	5	8	60
Ohio	633	730	10
Oklahoma	253	280	11
Oregon	108	85	−21
Pennsylvania	801	740	−7
Rhode Island	48	48	0
South Carolina	390	395	1
South Dakota	14	4	−71

continued

TABLE 1.2
Continued

State	1990	1991	% Change
Tennessee	511	585	14
Texas	2,389	2,690	12
Utah	52	43	−17
Vermont	13	22	69
Virginia	545	550	1
Washington	238	240	1
West Virginia	102	95	−9
Wisconsin	225	290	30
Wyoming	22	22	0

SOURCE: U.S. Senate Judiciary Committee (1991).

Brown, Esbensen, and Geis (1991) state that in Detroit the risk of being a homicide victim is 1 in 27; in El Paso, it is 1 in 215 (p. 536). The risk of fatal violence is further complicated by gang activity, drug activity, and other social variables.

Murder rates can also vary among different parts of a particular city. In a classic study conducted in Philadelphia, Wolfgang and Ferracuti (1967) found that rates of homicide were highest in business districts and in lower-class districts.

WEAPONS USED

Weapons are used in homicides for the express purpose of fatally injuring victims. When a gun is used as a threat in other crimes of violence, seldom is the victim actually assaulted with the weapon; when a knife is used, it typically serves only as a means of intimidation (Jamieson & Flanagan, 1988; Vito & Holmes, 1993).

Handguns are the most popular weapons used in homicide: 43% of all murders involve the use of a handgun. Some form of firearm is present in 59% of homicides. Knives or other weapons used to stab or cut are used 21% of the time (Jamieson & Flanagan, 1988, p. 20).

Weapons Used in Homicides (in percentages)	
Firearms	64
Cutting or stabbing weapons	18
Blunt objects	5
Personal (hand, foot, fist, etc.)	7
Other (poison, fire, explosives)	2
Unknown	4

SOURCE: U.S. Department of Justice, BJS (1991b, p. 398).

GENERAL TYPOLOGIES OF MURDERERS

Each chapter of this book discusses a certain type of homicide. Within each type of killing—partner homicide, mass murder, serial murder, and so on—unique typologies are offered. However, before we enter into in-depth examination of these types, we want to mention some more general types that may or may not exactly fit the typologies offered within the individual chapters.

Some killers are of the *depressive* type. These murderers seldom have police or criminal records. Often they are under the care of mental health practitioners and are not considered sociopathic or psychopathic. They may believe that life is hopeless and not worth living. Such individuals are not only likely to commit suicide but also to take loved ones with them. They view their acts of murder subjectively as acts of love. (For a more detailed analysis of the depressive personality, the reader is referred to Emile Durkheim's discussions of anomie.)

Another type of killer is the *mysoped,* the sadistic child offender. These individuals connect the act of murder, particularly of children, with sexual gratification (Holmes, 1983). Many cases of such murderers are well documented and are well known to the public. William Hatcher killed as many as 5 children, mainly in Missouri, in the 1970s (Gainey, 1989). Wayne Williams at one time was considered to be the killer of as many as 26 black children in Atlanta (Dettlinger, 1983). Ottis Toole and Henry Lucas both confessed to the murders of several young children and to performing bizarre sexual acts on the children both prior to and after the murders (Hickey, 1991).

The *sexual killer* is often a serial killer. In Chapter 6 we examine the sexual sadist extensively. We note here only that sexual killers connect sexual violence and murder with personal sexual gratification, and, because of this, they are likely to be serial offenders (Hickey, 1991; Holmes, 1989).

The *psychotic killer* crosses several offender types. Such persons have lost contact with reality and often experience hallucinations or hear voices. For example, Joseph Kallinger, known as "the Shoemaker," heard a voice that commanded him to kill everyone in the entire world (Schreiber, 1984). Kallinger has been diagnosed as a psychotic individual by those in the mental health profession, and he is still a danger to society. He has been quoted as saying that he will kill again if he gains his freedom. He still sees "Charlie," the head that he says spoke to him and told him to kill (Schreiber, 1984).

One category that encompasses many of the various types of killers discussed in this book is that of the *psychopathic killer.* Ted Bundy, John Gacy, Henry Lucas, and many other serial homicidal offenders can be described as psychopathic. A psychopathic individual has a character disorder that results in his or her being unable to experience feelings of social responsibility, guilt, shame, empathy, sorrow, or any of the other "normal" feelings that generally result when one has harmed another person. The psychopathic killer is concerned only with his or her own feelings. To illustrate, we offer the following statement, which is part of a letter written to the first author by a psychopathic offender currently in prison in California.

I enjoyed killing.

Yes, that's correct. I actually enjoyed killing. I enjoyed killing young females. Slender ones. Cheerleader types. The prettier the better. For me, there was no greater thrill, no greater high, and no greater meaning than that which I derived from holding in the palm of my hand the life of just such a creature, a young woman unable to resist or flee, and then slowly destroying that same life for my own personal pleasure. Ritualistic games of torture. Good old fashioned rape. Then murder. It was always quite fun. Unimaginably gratifying. Fulfilling.

Someone listening to our conversation may well find it abhorrent for me to be expressing such an apparent fondness for sadism and cold blooded murder. Some may even call it madness.

Others may call it evil. Or some may call it a grotesque sickness beyond the understanding of psychiatry's most expert minds. But, regardless of the label, one might wish to place upon me or my past behavior, there is no denying the fact that this deliberate snuffing out of human life was once no less than a refreshing and regular pastime for me. As natural to me as breathing air or eating food. As thoroughly satisfying as an ice cold beer on a wretchedly hot afternoon. And were I not locked away inside a prison cell this moment, there's no question about what I might otherwise be doing to occupy my hours this very same winter's night.

Perhaps even now, I might be behind a friendly smile, trading laughter with some unsuspecting stranger—a young attractive hitchhiker, or maybe a shy, unwary schoolgirl—while my brain concentrated hard on maintaining a winsome masquerade of normalcy. Even now, I might be luring such a creature into her place of doom, my guts churning with the anticipation of feeding upon the terror, the misery, and the certain demise I'd soon be bringing to bear upon my hapless captive-to-be. This very minute, I might well be strangling or beating away forever the life of yet another innocent human being—even as I did so often, so brutally, and so remorselessly throughout a long, dark chapter of my hideous past.

Obviously, I won't be killing anybody's daughter or sister this evening, and it is certain that I'll never be given the opportunity to do so again in the future. Still, it must be rather evident by now, that before I was captured and condemned to live out the rest of my life behind prison walls, I was not much different from such well-known and often psychopaths as Kenneth Bianchi, Angelo Buono, Christopher Wilder, or Ted Bundy. Like each of these men, serial killers, all of them—I, too, once roamed the streets in pursuit of human prey, luring one young woman after another to a grisly death. Like them, I killed repeatedly and without mercy, without the slightest trace of conscience. Like all of these men, I, too, was a serial killer.

Serial killer. Most people clothe their images of serial killers with only their deepest negative feelings of contempt and loathing. "Just catch the murderous bastards!" is a common refrain among society at large, "then fry their asses in the electric chair and let them all rot in hell forever!" Certainly, this attitude is not a surprise, as no one knows better than I do that a serial killer is indeed a horrifying specter, a living nightmare run amok. And, even while a serial killer actually is very much a human being— someone whose life begins just like any other life—I think it perfectly natural that most law-abiding citizens just don't give a damn about HOW or WHY such a man should come one day to strike terror in the hearts of so many.

Understanding, then, it is extremely difficult for those who have never once entertained the idea of killing a fellow human being to consider even for a moment that NO MAN—not even one as famously heinous as a Ted Bundy—is born into this world with an inherited desire to destroy the lives of others. Yet, if a serial killer's life does indeed begin just like any other, and if he, like everyone else, leaves his mother's womb in a state of innocence, completely untouched by murderous inclinations, then isn't this evidence enough that serial killers will continue making their deadly appearance on the American scene for as long as birthed into existence? And with this in mind, is it not pure folly to recoil away from learning all of the HOWS and WHYS behind such a person's escalation from childhood innocence to monstrous deeds of violence in adulthood.

Many years have passed since my own killing career was brought to a stop, and this prison cell wherein I now sit is literally the end of the line for me. But, while it only heightens my awareness of a desolate future to write about my past as a serial killer, I nevertheless begin this talk with you this afternoon with a sense of having no other choice but to do so. I realize few people would ever believe that I now despise what I became, or that I deeply regret the mountain of suffering and grief for which I am directly responsible. Yet, I also know that I was not the first man to haunt the streets and neighborhoods of Anytown, USA, targeting for slaughter the lives of innocent human beings—nor am I destined to be the last of my kind to do the same. And if there is to be any hope of identifying and then preventing budding, would-be serial killers from maturing into full-fledged beasts of destruction, I am convinced that this will happen only through understanding the secret inner workings of people like myself.

This serial killer has, by his own admission, killed scores of innocent people. He possesses a character defect that renders him incapable of sorrow, regret, or even wishing to stop his victimization. He stated that he does not like what he has done to others, "but don't let me out because if you do I'll kill again and more viciously than before."

Some murderers kill because they have *organic* or *brain disorders* that make them prone to violence (Norris, 1988).

Some researchers, such as Norris (1988), believe firmly that certain kinds of physical dysfunctions in individuals can account for their violence, whether resulting from a blow to the head or from the presence in men of an extra Y chromosome, a theory that was brought to public attention in the 1960s with the case of Richard Speck, who murdered eight student nurses in Chicago. (Actually, Speck was found not to have an extra Y chromosome, but this has not deterred Norris, who asserts that the root cause of criminality and violence lies solely in the biological realm. Despite his best efforts, this theory has not been validated.)

Some killers are *mentally retarded.* The homicides these murderers commit are often not carried out in ways that are typical of most other killers. The mentally retarded killer will kill to cover up abnormal acts, sometimes sexual acts, sometimes accidents.

Other killers murder for reasons that have nothing to do with the various motives cited above. These are *professional hit* killers; they assassinate complete strangers for economic, political, or ideological reasons. Chapter 4, on hate crimes, and Chapter 7, on terrorism, examine this type of killer.

CONCLUSION

Senator Joseph Biden, chairman of the U.S. Senate Judiciary Committee, has stated that increases in the murder rate are fueled by the "three Ds": drugs and drug dealers; deadly arsenals, particularly assault weapons; and demographics, including the growth in violent teen gangs (Squiteri, 1991). Whatever the causes, it is clear that violence plays an important role in the lives of many North Americans, and that too often this violence takes the form of murder. The many facets and characteristics of this fatal violence are the focus of the remainder of this book.

As we have shown, there is no one single reason for killing. The motivations, methods, and selections of victims are as different as the personalities of the killers themselves. Murder is a complex behavior. For some who kill, murder is utilitarian; for others, it is instrumental, the result of an impulse, or a response to a psychological need. The following chapters examine different types of murderers and their motivations.

2

Partner Homicide

There is a thin line between love and hate. There may be an even finer line between love and violence within a family setting. This line is too often transgressed and domestic violence ensues, sometimes resulting in the tragedy of homicide.

Why a relationship between two partners who have committed their lives together may turn violent (or why it is violent from the beginning) is not well understood, although many studies have examined the characteristics of both abused partners and their abusers (see, e.g., Gelles, 1974, 1979; Gelles & Straus, 1989; Hansen & Harway, 1993). Some researchers are convinced that wife abuse in particular is a further manifestation of society's general devaluation of and violence against women (see, e.g., Stordeur & Stille, 1989). In any case, although they differ as to estimates, most researchers agree that spouse abuse is underreported by victims—to law enforcement, to spouse abuse centers, and to other agencies that deal with this significant issue. The data that are available for examination are solely from the cases that are known, and these may be only the tip of the iceberg.

This chapter examines partner homicide, or the killing of one spouse by the other. Although most people think of the family as a safe, emotionally warm setting, an atmosphere of safety for

18

all members, this is unfortunately not always the case. We present some statistics on the prevalence of spouse abuse and partner homicide below, and then we examine the law enforcement and judicial system responses to this form of homicide.

STATISTICS ON SPOUSAL HOMICIDE

Staggering statistics enumerated in popular magazines and professional journals attest to the problem of fatal partner violence. These statistics have been gathered by serious researchers who are attempting to examine the true extent of the problem and some possible solutions (Ewing, 1987; Gelles & Pedrick-Cornell, 1983; Goetting, 1987, 1989; Hagaman, Wells, & Blau, 1987; Kalichman, 1988; Smith, 1989; Straus & Gelles, 1986). Each year in the United States, thousands of people are abused and battered by their spouses. One study estimates that in more than 50% of all marriages, the couples have experienced at least one incident of assault (Feld & Straus, 1989). Fortunately, not all of these cases result in deaths.

Recent studies on partner homicide suggest that the problem exists on an international scale. For example, in Quebec, Canada, 30 women a year are killed by their partners (Came & Bergman, 1990). In England, every three days a woman is killed by her husband or boyfriend (Smith, 1989, p. 1). In the United States, a woman is more likely to be assaulted, injured, raped, or killed by a male partner than by a stranger (Browne & Williams, 1987). According to Mann (1988), nearly 70% of incidents of domestic violence are committed by husbands, boyfriends, or ex-boyfriends. This estimate is reinforced by the work of Carmody and Williams (1987), who found that in one five-year period (1980-1984), 52% of adult women who were murdered in a one-to-one homicide were killed by a husband, ex-husband, common-law husband, or boyfriend.

Some researchers have attempted to compile statistics on the incidence of partner homicide. Using data from the Federal Bureau of Investigation's *Supplemental Homicide Reports* for the years 1976 to 1985, Mercy and Saltzman (1989) identify 16,595 partner homicides, accounting for 8.8% of all homicides:

The rate of spouse homicide for this ten year period was 1.6 per 100,000 married persons. The risk of being killed by one's spouse was 1.3 times greater for wives than for husbands. Black husbands were at greater risk of spouse homicide than black wives or white spouses of either sex. From 1976 through 1985, the risk of spouse homicide declined by more than 45.0 percent for both black husbands and wives but remained relatively stable for white husbands and wives.

One sad element in many partner homicides is that often the police have been called several times previously to the homes in which fatalities later occur (Buzawa & Buzawa, 1990). Our own communications with veteran police officials from several states throughout the United States indicate that in 80-95% of partner homicides, the police had been called to the home at least once during the two years preceding the incident. In more than half of these cases, they had been called five times or more. We found in interviewing women in Kentucky's maximum security prison that 40% of inmates who were incarcerated for murder or manslaughter had killed their partners who had repeatedly assaulted them. These women had sought police protection numerous times before re-sorting to murder. One prison official estimated that 9 of 10 women who killed their mates had been battered by them. In the majority of cases, the murders resulted from the women's attempts to protect themselves or their children (Doris Stephens, personal communication, May 1992).

One young woman, Linda H, 21 years old, was arrested and sentenced to 25 years in a Kentucky prison for the murder of her common-law husband.[1] She related her story to the first author:

I was first married when I was 17. It wasn't a good marriage and Tom and I got divorced in a year. But I already had Bobby [her son] when we broke up.

Me and John met up a month after I left Tom. John was no good. He was a drug dealer and a coke head. I knew that when I moved in with him, but I did it anyhow.

Things were a little rough, really, from the beginning. He hit me a few times, and I would just take it. He was good to Bobby, so I thought it would all turn out all right.

One night, he got high and started to hit on me. He then hit Bobby and threw him across the room against the wall. Something just snapped in me. It was one thing for him to hit me. I wasn't going to let him beat up on Bobby. So I went into the bedroom and got his gun and shot him. He moved, and I shot him again.

No, I'm not sorry. I miss my son. He's staying with my parents until I get out. I just couldn't let him beat up on Bobby. Could I?

It appears that only a small percentage of battered women kill their abusers to end the violence. Some are eventually able to leave their abusive relationships, and some go on suffering, unable to break the cycle of violence or to leave. There is no way to gauge accurately the number of women, or men, who are involved in abusive partnerships and never resort to fatal violence. There are many who are "in the closet" and never make the abuse public. What is known, however, is that the number appears to be rising (Gelles & Straus, 1985).

WHO IS AT RISK?

In domestic relationships the roles and interactions between the two partners are complex. Nonetheless, it is important to understand the nature of a relationship in order to evaluate it. Roles such as husband and wife, friend and lover, are complex. Behavioral expectations and anticipated gains can be unclear and difficult to sort out. However, when partners' expectations of their relationship are not fulfilled, violence can result. The manifestation of that violence is bordered by the moral and legal responses that exist in society. In other words, societal responses to those who resort to fatal domestic violence can set the tone for the continued exercise of violence by others or for its diminishment. We must examine the motivations, potential gains, and potential losses incurred by those who commit partner homicide in order to understand this phenomenon.

For years, too many assumptions have been made regarding the relationships, motivations, and anticipated gains that result in partner violence. For example, many have assumed, erroneously, that both partners are at equal risk for domestic homicide. Research indicates that there are definite gender differences in risk level: Women are at greater risk of being killed by their spouses than are men (Kratcoski, 1987). The physical strength of the male is only one possible explanation. Men, for example, are more likely than women to have high stress scores on psychometric scales (Kratcoski, 1987). The source of the stress is more likely to have resulted from traumatic losses in the men's lives (health or job) or other very painful experiences. These losses or experiences occur typically before the homicidal incident (Kratcoski, 1987). On the other hand, homicides committed by women against their spouses are more likely to be linked to domestic stress and are often preceded by a history of wife abuse. In the cases of both husbands and wives, it appears that those who resort to fatal violence within the family are unable to respond adequately to high levels of stress (Kratcoski, 1987).

In dealing with the stress of repeated abuse at the hands of their spouses, many women exhibit uniform behavioral and psychological responses to their perceived (and, in most cases, real) dangerous reality. The outcome of these perceptions is an accumulation of a great deal of anger, which is not always directed toward the abuser. In many cases, abused women direct their anger inward, and it manifests in suicidal behavior, poor self-image, drug abuse, and alcoholism; on rare occasions it may take the form of stigmatophilia (self-mutilation) (Fishbain, Rao, & Aldrich, 1985; Lester, 1987).

WHERE THE CRIMES OCCUR

In partner homicide, there are interesting differences between the sexes as to where the murders tend to occur. One reason may lie in the availability of the weapons used. Routine activity theory may play an important role in the site as well as the weapon used in partner homicide (Messner & Tardiff, 1985). In almost 9 cases out of 10, the act of spouse homicide occurs in the home (Browne, 1986; Kratcoski, 1987). The location of the murder within the home appears to be related to where the individuals spend the most time or where they most often come into confrontation. Mann (1988), for example, found that women who commit partner homicide are most likely to kill in the living room; next most likely is the bedroom, and then the kitchen. Men who kill their partners, however, do not show any such pattern.

WEAPONS USED

The methods and weapons used in partner homicide vary widely: knives, guns, poisons, rifles, blunt instruments, asphyxiation, and explosives have all been used, as have the murderer's bare hands. Handguns are often readily available, and this has caused some to question how much this availability itself might contribute to the incidence of spousal murder (Browne, 1987). Some proponents of gun control, for example, stress the importance of some form of legislation regarding the purchase of handguns as one method of reducing partner homicides. There are conflicting opinions on this issue, of course. Howard (1986) has examined the gun control issue from the perspective of family law. Considering that in most cases of partner homicide a firearm is used, she reports two interesting suppositions:

1. Spousal homicides are spontaneous "crimes of passion" that result from momentary rages arising from the heat of circumstances, rather than from a fixed determination to kill. (p. 64)
2. If deprived of guns, spouse killers either would not substitute another weapon or would substitute a weapon less lethal than a gun. (p. 66)

From this perspective, gun control legislation would have a direct impact on the rate of spouse homicides, at least for those committed by males. Research findings concerning the impact such legislation would have on the rate of spouse killings by women are unclear, however. Research has shown that often women who kill their husbands use knives (in part because of the place-specific nature of the weapon used, and the fact that many such homicides take place in the kitchen).

For women in precarious living situations, the gun may indeed be "the great equalizer." For example, a woman using a knife as a murder weapon exposes herself to a greater risk of successful resistance by her male partner, because she must approach within arm's length of him. Removing the gun from her hand and replacing it with a knife may render her defense ineffective and result in her becoming the victim, perhaps with fatal consequences. Browne (1986) notes that 81% of women who kill their abusive mates use guns; knives are the weapons in such cases only 7% of the time.

Men who kill their spouses do not show a preference for any one kind of weapon. For men, the murder weapon may be incidental to the motivation of the killer and the location of the attack.

PERPETRATOR PROFILES

Women Who Kill

Although some women do kill their spouses for other reasons, apparently most who do so are responding to some form of victim-precipitated attack. Often, these women have histories of long-term abuse at the hands of the men they kill (Mann, 1988). Goetting (1987), who studied 56 women arrested for spousal homicide in Detroit between 1982 and 1983, lists the following characteristics in a profile of female killers:

- black
- early or mid-30s
- a mother
- lived with family
- uneducated
- unemployed
- prior arrest record

According to Goetting's profile, these women kill after a series of heated arguments or volatile confrontations with their slightly older partners. The final argument typically takes place in the bedroom or living room, between 2:00 p.m. and the very early morning hours. The image that emerges from the research is one of a woman who is disadvantaged along several dimensions, including a sense of social isolation. These minority women live in loosely structured relationships with men and are poorly equipped to succeed in their daily struggles to survive in society. They are mired in a world in which they have few social, educational, and personal strengths to rise beyond their limited social level. The women are viewed as victims in a male-dominated world, in a society that is structured to be conducive to success for men.

Characteristics of Battered Women Who Kill

- sufferers of frequent and severe verbal abuse
- victims of often brutal assaults
- threatened frequently with death
- history of suicide attempts
- better educated than their partners
- living apart from their partners

SOURCE: Barnard, Vera, Vera, and Newman (1982).

Browne (1987) notes other characteristics of women involved in partner homicide. Many women in her sample of more than 300 came from families in which they were themselves abused as children, typically by their fathers. This same finding is reported by Korbin (1986) and Conway (1989). Ironically, these women later married husbands who were similar in personality traits to their fathers. These researchers also note several "predictors" of women's resorting to fatal violence in a domestic setting:

- the severity of the woman's injuries
- the man's drug use and frequency of intoxication
- the frequency of abuse
- forced or threatened sexual acts by the man
- suicidal threats by the woman
- threats to kill made by the man

Women may blame themselves when placed in a situation of partner homicide. According to statistics, only a small number of women involved in domestic abuse ever resort to homicide as a resolution for what they see as a hopeless position. Women who are the victims of long-term abuse tend to develop feelings of helplessness and anomie, which make it even more difficult for them to fight back (Walker, 1979, 1989). Also, the marriages of battered women tend to adhere to strict gender roles, with the men being domineering and the women submissive (see, e.g., Hansen & Harway, 1993; Stordeur & Stille, 1989). It may be that these women strike back only when they see no other way to end their suffering. In essence, it may be that many women kill as a fatalistic and final response to unrelenting violence within a family setting.

Researchers such as Lenore Walker (1979, 1989) have described the cycle that spouse abuse, most often wife abuse, typically follows. Each incident of abuse may be divided into three stages. The first stage, the prebattering period, is a time of increasing strain between the victim and the batterer. The abuser may make verbal assaults, attack inanimate objects (especially the victim's possessions or other items she values), and engage in minor acts of violence against the victim. The victim may respond by trying to calm or placate the abuser. The goal is to defuse the potentially dangerous situation.

If the nonbattering partner is successful, the matter will stop here. However, if this fails, or if the anger is too great, the second stage, violence, will occur. Here both parties have lost control of the situation. The batterer lashes out in a rage, often causing serious injury. The victim too has lost control. The abuse can only be endured at this time.

In the last stage, with his rage spent and the victim showing obvious injuries, the batterer tries to console the victim. He may beg for forgiveness, promise to try to resolve the problem (e.g., to quit drinking or to avoid certain people or situations), or promise to seek counseling. These conciliatory gestures rarely endure, however, and soon the cycle starts again.

A woman is more likely to leave an abusive relationship once the rate of positive reinforcement (the promises made in the third stage in the cycle) decreases. This point of separation, once reached, is risky for both partners. It poses such a threat of abandonment that a man may kill his partner rather than let her leave. Conversely, a man who prevents his partner's leaving may jeopardize his own life. In these cases, it is the woman who turns on her mate during an attempt to escape, never intending to kill but only to prevent him from blocking her escape or to keep him from hurting her again.

There indeed may be a "paralyzing terror" in the relationship at this point. As noted earlier, battered women build up high levels of anger, but they "rarely experience their anger directly"

(Howard, 1986, p. 77). Although they most often direct their aggression inward and appear to be passive receivers of their abuse, "passivity and denial of anger do not imply that the battered woman is adjusted to or likes the situation. It is the last defense against homicidal rage" (p. 77).

Men Who Kill

Men who kill their partners typically have been found to be quiet, to want to be accepted by society despite their homicidal acts, but to be unable to relate to the world around them, and to exhibit a great deal of daily stress in their lives (Smith, 1989). Often men involved in partner homicide were reared in a tradition of "keeping a stiff upper lip" in the face of personal adversity. These men also have a great deal of difficulty expressing their emotions (Smith, 1989).

According to Humphrey and Palmer (1987), homicide offenders are more apt to have experienced considerable losses throughout their lives; parents died or were separated from them by divorce, abandonment, or institutionalization. Later in life they experienced difficulties on the job, changed residences frequently, and often went through changes in marital status. These stressful events can combine to spark homicidal attacks, usually on persons the offenders fear losing the most, such as a spouse, a child, or a close friend.

Perhaps men who feel unable to control their own lives outside the family are particularly likely to exert control within the family. One person such a man may be able to control is his female partner. As Sylvie Schrim, a Montreal attorney, stated, "I am continually dealing with men who want to control the women in their lives, who view their partners as some kind of property" (quoted in Came & Bergman, 1990, p. 18). If such a man is placed in a situation where his partner is striving for personal autonomy (which he perceives to be at his expense), whether within the relationship or by leaving the relationship, he may see violence as his sole answer to the problem. Killing, here, may be seen as an act of control.

Long-lasting periods of stress become an integral part of the psychologically impelling "compulsion" to lash out fatally. This point is illustrated by Humphrey and Palmer (1987), who report that men who become murderers often do so as a result of prolonged frustration. In their sample, they found the lives of the killers to be more stressful than the lives of the nonkillers, and the stress was endured over a longer period of time.

Weiner, Zahn, and Sagi (1990) note that there are significant differences between men who commit partner homicide and men in the general noncriminal population. For instance, men who kill their partners are more often drug abusers, are more prone to abuse alcohol and are intoxicated more often, and are more frequently given to verbalizing physical threats and exhibiting violent forms of physical behavior than are other men. Tragically, men who murder their wives are also more likely to have been abused themselves as children, emotionally, physically, and sexually. Such men are also more likely to commit sexual violence against their partners than are males not involved in partner homicide.

THE LAW AND LEGAL DEFENSES IN CASES OF SPOUSAL HOMICIDE[2]

The law does not regulate behavior in a social vacuum. There are performers in this arena of criminal justice who all play vital roles. Historically, wives were viewed as the property of their husbands, to do with as they so desired (see, e.g., U.S. Commission on Civil Rights, 1982). The laws have changed radically in this area, reflecting a changing sense of priorities and fairness. The U.S. Attorney General's Task Force on Family Violence (1984) recommends that the determination to take legal action should be guided more by the form of abuse and less by the relationship between the abuser and the victim. This statement has been construed to extend beyond the "traditional" family to nontraditional relationships as well.

Law Enforcement

The police officer on the beat is usually the first to respond to the domestic disturbance call. The common reaction for many officers in the past was to separate the quarreling couple, diminish the hostility, and simply allow the two people to "cool off." For years this approach was part of the "prevailing wisdom" on domestic violence. However, in many cases where the police took this approach, sometimes returning to a particular residence on more than five separate occasions, the situation was not improved, and the end result was partner homicide. Now, many jurisdictions have adopted a different strategy. In Kentucky, for example, the police may make an arrest even if the battered spouse chooses not to prosecute. If the officer believes a danger exists to one partner from the other, this provides the needed justification for intervention (Douglas Hamilton, chief of police, Louisville, Kentucky, Police Department, personal communication, March 30, 1993).

It is estimated that as many as half of all cases of partner abuse that later result in partner homicide are never reported. Clearly, a concentrated effort needs to be made to improve the reporting of such violence, and for this we need a greater understanding of the reasons behind the failure to report. Some victims, for example, may not report abuse because of fear of personal reprisals or the negative stigma attached to such a public admission. Others may not report abuse because of possible repercussions for their status in the community or their positions in the workplace. Despite the many possible reasons for victims' reluctance to report their abuse, those who are involved in potentially fatal relationships clearly need to be encouraged to do so.

One further note on this issue: The police have historically been reticent to respond to domestic disturbance calls. Horror stories are continually told of the personal risks to officers involved in such calls—risks of injury and even death. However, our own data analysis indicates that police officers actually are at greater personal risk in responding to robbery calls than in responding to domestic disturbances.

Prosecutors

The National Woman Abuse Prevention Project concerns itself especially with the relatively low rate of spouse abuse cases that are reported and then later prosecuted. Perhaps this low rate is a reflection of the previously common position taken in society that what goes on within the domestic sphere, even abuse (which may later turn to partner homicide), is a private concern best left to the parties involved to resolve. Whatever the reasons, prosecutors frequently fail to send spouse abuse cases forward for judicial deliberation. Some prosecutors believe that domestic violence is a low-priority issue, and that all a couple needs is a "cooling off" period. Violence between spouses is often not viewed in the same manner as violence between two strangers. Some prosecutors even discourage battered partners (male or female) from seeking judicial deliberation. They may either deliberately or unintentionally belittle the merits of these cases and thus convince the victims that they have little chance of successful resolution.

Some prosecutors may see cases of domestic violence as having relatively low priority in comparison with other crimes. They may plea-bargain cases involving serious battering down to misdemeanor status. This sends a message to those who batter that this type of crime is not taken too seriously by those in the legal system. Because the cases are not prosecuted as diligently as they should be, offenders are too often released from custody to return to commit yet more acts of abuse, and sometimes partner homicide is the consequence.

It is also the case that some victims simply refuse to testify against their abusers, because of fear of reprisals, reluctance to share intimate secrets of their lives, and other reasons.

From a prosecutorial posture there are no easy steps to follow in order to achieve a successful resolution in a battering case. There is no magic wand to wave to protect the abused and to prevent further abuse. However, certain key elements of a successful prosecutorial response have been identified. After these guidelines were implemented in San Francisco, the National Woman Abuse Prevention Project reported a 44% increase in the conviction rate of felony cases, a 136% increase in the number of cases in which charges are filed, and a 171% increase in the disposition of domestic violence cases there (Soler, 1987). Greater success in intervention by the criminal justice system in abuse cases should sharply reduce the number of partner homicides committed.

The Judicial Response

In domestic violence and partner homicide cases, as in all court cases, judges have the primary role of ensuring that the law is followed. However, judges also are involved in the often highly subjective task of sentencing, and in cases of spouse abuse the sentences they pass sometimes reflect their own ignorance of the severity and the potential for escalation of domestic violence.

There is a common assumption that all judges are wise, analytical, and learned. Unfortunately, this is not always the case. Too few judges who must preside over cases of domestic violence are cognizant of the intricacies of human behavior. Their educational training has been focused on the law, and for the most part any education they may have had in human behavior came in their undergraduate years, in introductory psychology and sociology courses. The psychology of the spouse batterer, and of the partner murderer, is complex. When judges apply the dictates of the law without firm grounding in the nuances of such human behavior, a great disservice is done to society and to the victims of domestic violence in particular.

Too many judges are ignorant of the nature of partner homicide as well as the antecedent behaviors of physical, emotional, and sexual abuse. Because of this ignorance, which comes out of academic deficiencies and, in more than a few cases, personal prejudices, many judges fail to realize the seriousness of the problem of abuse. The light sentences for abusers that can result from judicial ignorance may themselves make possible later acts of homicide.

The Law and Partner Homicide

The task of defending in court a woman who has killed an abusive spouse is formidable. In many such cases, the men posed no immediate threat to the women at the time of the killings, yet the women will insist that they killed in self-defense. Self-defense laws generally require a perception of imminent danger, and they do not take into consideration the reasonableness of

the prediction of imminent danger based on a history of repeated acts of violence (Simpson, 1989; Walker, 1993). Psychologists disagree with this legal standard and argue that battered women may reasonably expect their husbands' anger to
escalate quickly because experience has taught them to recognize cues of pending abuse. Many argue that being the victim of
years of abuse can lead to a person's showing symptoms not
unlike those found in post-traumatic stress disorder; this has
been called *battered woman syndrome* (Walker, 1983, 1984,
1989). In recent years, some states have allowed a legal defense
in such cases called "battered woman self-defense," which is
based on the premise that a woman suffering from battered
woman syndrome may perceive herself to be in danger when no
imminent threat is apparent (Walker, 1993).

Currently, the self-defense statutes in most states also include
equal force requirements, which assume that the parties to a
physical struggle are of equal size and have equal experience
with using parts of their bodies to defend themselves. Hence
when a battered woman uses a weapon to defend herself against
a physically stronger man who uses fists, her legal accountability
raises from a misdemeanor to a felony. However, because women
are in general smaller than men and are not socialized to defend
themselves physically as men are, weapons may be seen as
necessary elements in women's self-protection.

Public policy regarding domestic violence has changed greatly
in the past decade, and psychologists have played an active role
in this transformation. Court testimony by expert witnesses has
refuted many myths about domestic violence, such as that battered women are masochistic and stay with their mates because
they like to be beaten, that violence fills a deep-seated need that
attracts partners to each other, and that because battered women
have free will they can leave a relationship if they only choose
to do so. These myths have prevented battered women who kill
their abusers from receiving impartial trials.

Since 1986, expert testimony on battered woman syndrome
has been allowed in cases of women accused of killing their
partners in more than 20 states. Admission of such testimony has
been denied in Wyoming, Ohio, Florida, and Missouri. This
prohibition is being appealed in Missouri and Florida, and recently testimony has been permitted in similar circumstances in

these two states (Soler, 1987). The first step for a defense attorney representing a woman who has killed a partner is to determine whether, in fact, the case involved battering. This is crucial for the introduction of battered woman syndrome as an element in the defense.

Many states do not have self-defense laws, and in those states even the belief that one is in dire or fatal danger is not considered an adequate defense for the commission of homicide. Even in a state where self-defense may be recognized, "perfect" self-defense requires that the perpetration of fatal violence was necessary and reasonable. If a person's attempt at self-defense is deemed to have involved "unnecessary or excessive" force, then he or she cannot be freed on grounds of self-defense. If the amount of force used in self-defense is found to be "necessary and reasonable," even if it resulted in the death of the attacker, then it is deemed to be "perfect" self-defense, and there is no finding of guilt.

Sometimes the outgrowth of a self-defense plea is a finding of "imperfect" self-defense; this is often the case in findings of manslaughter. The case of *State v. Thorton* (1987) provides an example. In this case, a man came home unexpectedly and found his wife in bed with another man, whom the husband then killed. He was convicted of first-degree murder. The charge was later reduced to voluntary manslaughter because the court found that (a) there was adequate provocation, which caused (b) extreme anger and rage ("In our opinion, the passions of any reasonable person would have been inflamed and intensely aroused by this sort of discovery."), (c) there was no opportunity to cool off, and (d) there was a causal connection between the provocation, anger, and the fatal act. Legal precedent has established the circumstances under which men and women may react with fatal force as well as how the courts perceive that behavior.

It is unclear what, if any, particular direction the courts are taking in deciding cases of domestic violence. Some legal decisions point toward a relatively "classical" approach; others indicate a turning toward a philosophy that may be called the "medical model," which takes into account such concepts as battered woman syndrome, post-traumatic stress disorder, and battered woman self-defense. In some parts of the country, for example, women are incarcerated for partner homicide; in others they are granted probation or their cases are dismissed. In other words, there is a lack of consistency nationwide in the adjudication of partner homicide.

It should be noted that there are some researchers who claim that the character of partner homicide is changing. Wilbanks (1983), for instance, asserts that women who kill their partners are becoming more deliberate in their murder, that their extent of planning is more complex. If true, such a shift will have an influence on the law and on litigation in cases of partner homicide. Mann (1988), in a controversial conclusion, has gone so far as to state that women who kill may indeed be the victors in domestic fights and that the question of self-defense deserves reexamination.

POLICY IMPLICATIONS

Ideally, the criminal justice system operates smoothly and efficiently in dealing with the varying personalities, politics, and so on that enter into court cases. Too often, however, the system does not succeed. In one case in the early 1980s, for example, a young mother in a southern state was strangled to death by her partner. This attack occurred after her partner had perpetrated a series of increasingly violent attacks upon her. He was convicted of manslaughter rather than murder because the court decided that there was sufficient provocation to somehow mitigate the circumstances. He served less than five years in prison on this charge.

This was not the only time that this defendant had been before the court. Earlier, the court had issued an injunction against him, prohibiting him from having any contact with his partner; he promptly violated that injunction. He was arrested for that violation, but soon was released. His violent assaults upon the woman continued, but the system did little to aid her. Law enforcement's response to the increasing violence was ineffective. The woman was given no protection, and she died at the hands of this man despite the court's order prohibiting personal contact and despite the arrests made by the police. The case simply "fell through the cracks" and resulted in her brutal murder.

As noted above, the police traditionally have been reluctant to become involved in domestic disputes. Historically, the police have arrested abusers only if their victims have been willing to press charges. The law in many areas has now been changed to allow investigating officers to make the determination of abuse and act legally upon that determination. This is a positive step.

Sentencing in cases of spousal abuse has traditionally been light. Sometimes, prosecutors "undercharge" the perpetrators. In cases that do not result in death, often the victims decide not to pursue prosecution and cases are dropped. In still other cases, plea bargaining results in reduced charges.

Shelters for abused women are few and overcrowded, and many battered women simply have no place to go. Moreover, there are very few sources of social support for men who are battered. For an abused partner to return to the place where the battering has occurred in many cases means not only a continuation of the battering but a further escalation of the violence.

Solutions to the very serious and complex social problem of domestic violence are beyond the scope of this chapter. Clearly, however, both abusers and their victims are in need of education, as are those in law enforcement and the judicial system who must deal with the potentially fatal results of such violence. The police, typically the citizen's first line of entry into the criminal justice system, must be educated about the cycle of abuse and about such concepts as battered woman syndrome and victim blaming. The actors in the court system, from attorneys to judges, must also be made aware of the elements of psychology and complex human behavior involved in these cases so that they do not make judgments based upon myths and prejudices. Those in the corrections profession must also be informed of the problem of partner homicide and the special issues and behaviors presented in such cases.

CONCLUSION

Partner homicide and domestic violence in general are very complex, multifaceted problems. They are not well understood by the general public and, unfortunately, myths and misinformation surround them. Social and behavioral scientists are currently making important advances in the understanding of the problems of partner battering, domestic violence, and spousal homicide. All of the behavioral dynamics are still unclear, however, and there has been limited progress toward the ultimate goal—the solution of the social problem of partner abuse, which leads to homicide.

The mere treatment of the aftereffects of the violence perpetrated by one partner upon the other is insufficient. Better techniques need to be formulated that will result in early identification of both potential abusers, who may one day resort to fatal violence, and potential victims, who one day may be homicide statistics. Better education programs, more effective counseling techniques, and better understanding of the total problem are needed if there is to be an effective reduction in this most serious human condition, partner homicide.

NOTES

1. This woman's name has been changed to protect her privacy, as have the names of all prisoners quoted from our interview files throughout this book.
2. The discussion in this section is based for the most part on information found in the following sources: Attorney General's Task Force (1984), Cohn and Berk (1987), Garner and Clemmer (1985), Goolkasian (1986), Langan and Innes (1986), Lerman (1981), Police Foundation (1976), Sherman and Berk (1984), Soler (1987), and U.S. Commission on Civil Rights (1982).

3

Murder of Children

Those who kill children are held in particularly low esteem, not only in open society but in the prisons of our country as well. This is also true of those who physically or sexually abuse children. In Kentucky, a physician was recently found guilty of sexually abusing several of his young female patients. He was, unfortunately, granted probation by the sentencing judge, and one of the conditions of his probation was that he must move from his home community. He wanted to move to Florida, but the citizens of the small town there in which he owns a condominium mobilized a signature drive that was successful in blocking his move. At the time of this writing, he is exploring other areas to reside. This one case serves to illustrate the despised position of pedophiles in North America.

Those who victimize children are certainly viewed more harshly than are offenders who victimize adults. The thinking seems to be that adults who are victimized, especially within the family, have some "choice" and some ability to fight their own victimization, but that children are helpless and vulnerable. Parents who abuse their children are not uncommon. During his tenure as a probation officer, the first author came in contact with many such parents. One mother nailed her child to a cross on Good Friday, convinced that the child was the Baby Jesus, because she thought she was the Virgin Mary. In another case, a father was incarcerated for whipping his 14-year-old daughter with his leather belt. The daughter displayed the classic signs of an abused child: clinging to her father's side even in the courtroom, watching him for cues before she would speak or even move. She professed extreme love for her abusive father, as many abused children do, but even so, the father was sent to jail to consider his actions for the next year.

MURDER OF CHILDREN
IN THE UNITED STATES

We spoke with a killer of two small children who is currently in prison for their murders, and he told us that he has been violently victimized as an inmate. He said that only after he was struck in the head with an iron pipe in one incident did he have some realization of what it meant to be a victim. Other such offenders fear similar victimization. We interviewed a mother in Arkansas who had recently burned her child to death; she was fearful of going to jail because of what the women there would do to her. Another woman, a mother who had starved her child to death, complained of the manner in which she had been treated since she had been in prison, not only by the correctional personnel but also by the other residents. Apparently, the norms and values of free persons in society are little different from those of correctional residents when it concerns those who abuse children.

This chapter deals with individuals who fatally injure children. The first part of the chapter outlines the incidence of murder of children in general. We then examine the world of the aggressive and sexually sadistic child offender. Finally, we discuss parents and stepparents who kill their children, and some of the sociodemographic variables and characteristics that have been tied to such murderers.

FATAL CHILD ABUSE:
A GROWING CONCERN

In North America, child abuse within the family has not always been viewed as a paramount social issue. Nationwide polls in the United States conducted in the 1970s yielded results that seem almost unbelievable today. At that time, only 10% of the general population considered child abuse to be a serious problem. By 1983, this figure had risen to more than 90% (Wolfe, 1985). Numerous educational efforts are responsible for this rise in the public's social consciousness and the current judgment that the problem is a serious one.

Incidence of Physical and Fatal Child Abuse

Straus, Gelles, and Steinmetz (1980) estimated that in the latter part of the 1970s, 36 out of every 1,000 American children had experienced at least one "serious assault" at the hands of their parents or caretakers. In the early 1980s, Barry (1984) estimated that between 60,000 and 100,000 female children were being sexually abused within family settings. Moreover, he believed that 10% of American families were affected by incest. By 1990, conservative estimates were that at least 200,000 children are being physically abused within family settings (Gilbert, 1990, p. 416), and that more than 9 of 10 of these children are assaulted repeatedly. Straus and Gelles found in 1986 that the incidence of child abuse had actually diminished in the time since their previous study. They suggest that educational programs, increased social and legal sanctions, and knowledgeable social service agencies may have contributed to the decrease.

Each year in the United States, at least 1,000 children die from injuries inflicted by parents or other caretakers. Bartol (1991) estimates the number at 1,100. Even more are undoubtedly the victims of sadistic child offenders. The exact number who die this way, like the exact number who fall at the hands of parents or caretakers, is unknown. Regardless of how many die, and regardless of whether children are murdered by their parents or by strangers, it is clear that the killing of children is a genuine social problem. One murdered child is one too many. We cannot measure the importance of this problem simply in terms of numbers.

THE SADISTIC PEDOPHILE

Although it is generally believed that most pedophiles (adults who are sexually attracted to children) are not bent on directly harming their victims in a fatal fashion (Holmes, 1983), there are definitely some who connect sexual gratification with aggression and violence directed toward children. Westley Dodd, a convicted child killer, was such a pedophile. Recently executed in the state of Washington, Dodd had a long history of sexual paraphilias, including voyeurism and exhibitionism. This mysoped (or sadistic child offender) launched his killing career by murdering three small children, all boys. His first two victims were brothers whom he stabbed to death in a public park. The third victim was a 5-year-old he abducted from a school playground. In videotaped interviews, Dodd told police after his arrest that he took the boy to his apartment, later to a fast-food restaurant, and then to a discount store to buy him a toy. Enticing the youngster to spend the night with him, Dodd awoke his victim during the early morning hours and told him he was going to kill him. Climbing upon the bed, Dodd attempted to strangle the child. Unable to kill him with his hands, Dodd hanged him by the neck with a rope in a closet. Not wanting to be absent from work on the day a child was reported missing, Dodd hid the boy's body on a shelf in the closet and went to his job. When he returned to his apartment, he raped the boy's corpse before disposing of him.

Dodd was apprehended when he tried to abduct a fourth child. He was tried and sentenced to death. After his sentencing he became a familiar face on national TV talk shows. He stated that if he were free he knew that he would certainly continue to commit the same kinds of acts. He said on more than one occasion that he wanted to be executed. In a telephone conversation with the first author (December 21, 1992), he said that he felt he deserved to die, and that he knew he could not spend the rest of his life in prison.

Dodd's case is typical of sadistic child offenders. Albert Fish, an offender from the early part of the twentieth century known as the "moon maniac," is another example. Fish, an elderly, grandfatherly type, was finally arrested after years of careful investigation in New York. When they arrested him, police found body parts that apparently came from various children. Fish took his final victim, Grace Budd, from the Budd home under the pretense of taking her to attend a birthday party on Long Island. Taking her to an abandoned area, he killed her and then cooked portions of her body for his own consumption. More than a pedophile and a cannibal, Fish was also involved in infibulation, or self-torture of one's own sexual body parts. When he was executed in the electric chair at Sing Sing, the autopsy discovered 29 sewing needles implanted in his penis and scrotum (Schechter, 1990).

Other notable examples of adults who have murdered children include John Gacy, who killed 33 young men, most in their teens, and buried the majority in the crawl space under his home. Gacy sexually abused his victims both before and after their deaths, although he has consistently denied his guilt, stating that he was not aware of how those bodies got into his crawl space (Sullivan & Maiken, 1983). Gacy is currently on death row in Illinois. Henry Lucas and Ottis Toole both admitted to the murders of scores of victims, many of them children. Toole, currently in prison in Florida, at one time confessed to the murder of 7-year-old Adam Walsh (whose disappearance and murder were the subject of the 1983 television movie *Adam*), but he later recanted this confession.

The mysoped connects the violent sexual victimization of children, including fatal violence, with sexual gratification. Pedophiles of this ilk are likely to have extensive histories of antisocial behavior, as well as poor adaptation to social relationships. Most prefer victims of their own sex (Holmes, 1983, 1990). The more pain the mysoped inflicts, the greater the sense of gratification. This is graphically illustrated by Dodd's case; he kept a diary in which he wrote graphic descriptions of what he intended to do with his male victims: "exploratory surgery," anal sex, and body mutilations. When the murderous acts are successful, the mysoped becomes a serial killer of the type classified by Holmes and De Burger (1985) as hedonistic. Almost by definition, the sadistic child murderer is a serial offender. The child, usually unknown and abducted quickly, is tortured and often mutilated before being killed. Police have reported that the bodies of male victims often show evidence of gross acts of anal penetration, and that sometimes the penis is crudely amputated and inserted into the mouth. Female victims show evidence of violent acts directed toward the vaginal and anal cavities (Holmes, 1983). Obviously, the mysoped presents a very real danger to the children of this society.

PEDOPHILIA AND RECIDIVISM

National organizations exist that seek to legalize and validate pedophilic behaviors. The motto of one, the Rene Guyon Society, is "Sex before 8 or else it's too late!" That is, members believe that children should be sexually active before they are 8 years old. The North American Man/Boy Love Association lobbies for the enactment of legislation making sex with children legal. These agents for sexual change claim that there is little violence associated with sex between adults and children. As a matter of fact, they often assert that children are sexual aggressors, chasing adults until finally the adults consent to have sex with them. They cite studies done in the past to validate their point of view, and claim that children are full of body guilt, and if they will shed this body guilt they will grow into their adult years as fully functioning sexual beings. This presumption that sexual abstinence results in some form of personal pathology certainly lends credence to the legitimation of sex with children. If one believes such claims, then one could hardly be concerned about what otherwise would be viewed as serious acts of child molestation. Current research, however, does not support this view.

Early studies suggested that child molesters, both inside and outside the family, are serious recidivists. For example, Frisbie (1965) studied pedophiles in California and found that the rate of recidivism of heterosexual molesters was 18.2%. The rate for homosexual pedophiles was almost twice as high, 34.5%. However, these rates tell us very little about the total picture of child molesters and their crimes. As Schultz (1975) notes, most pedophile offenses go unreported. Abel, Becker, Murphy, and Flanagan (1981) report that the incarcerated homosexual pedophiles they studied had an average of 30 victims and that heterosexual pedophiles had an average of 62 victims. In another study, 14% of the sample admitted to sexual contacts with more than 50 children, and 6% reported having between 100 and 300 such contacts (Bernard, 1975).

Groth, Longo, and McFadin (1990), in an admirable study of sex offenders inside two correctional institutions in Florida and Connecticut, asked their subjects for the following details: the age of the offender at the time of his first sexual assault, the number of sexual assaults for which the offender had been convicted, the number of sexual assaults the offender had attempted or completed for which he was never apprehended, the number of sexual assaults the offender had been acquitted of, and, finally, the number of offenses for which he been found guilty but of which he was in fact innocent. The results of this study suggest that child sexual offenders avoid detection approximately twice as often as they are apprehended for their crimes. It should be noted that this conclusion was reached despite the fact that Groth et al. discarded several questionnaires because the subjects reported more than 50 incidents of molestation. Our own research indicates that such high numbers of molestations are not impossible, in any case. We have talked with several incarcerated pedophiles who also physically abused children who have each reported more than 30 occasions of abuse.

The molesters surveyed by Stermac, Hall, and Henskens (1989) claimed to believe that children were the real instigators in child abuse. However, current research indicates not only that this is untrue, but that there is a great deal of physical violence involved in such abuse. Stermac et al. also compared incest perpetrators with child molesters outside the family and found that the incest perpetrators were more violent in their dealings with children and that they used more verbal threats. Early work by DeFrancis (1969) showed that as many as 50% of all abusers had used varying degrees of physical violence in their abuse of children.

TREATMENT OF MYSOPEDS

One therapist we spoke with who is involved in the treatment of sexual offenders told us that she believes that, of all the types of sex offenders she deals with, pedophiles are the most difficult to treat (G. Spears, personal communication, May 19, 1991). Abel, Mittelman, Becker, Rathner, and Rouleau (1988) report that among all of the sex offenders in a treatment program they examined, pedophiles were least likely to complete the program (70%). In another analysis of treatment, Marshall and Barbaree (1988) studied a program that offered free counseling on a voluntary basis to sex offenders; 40% of the pedophiles refused to participate in this program. Of the ones who did participate, 14% completed the three-year program without officially reoffending.

It is commonly thought that behavior modification, aversion therapy, and group sessions have all provided less than ideal results with pedophiles. Pedophiles in general and mysopeds in particular have been with us for years, and we have little reason to believe that the problem will be solved. Children will continue to fall victim to adults who will sexually abuse them, some of whom are bent upon causing great physical pain and then death.

MURDER OF CHILDREN
WITHIN THE FAMILY

The family, usually thought of as a haven and a place of warmth and caring, can also be a setting for many different kinds of abuse. One type of abuse that is coming more and more to public attention but that is still little understood is incest. Homicide is rarely a direct result of incestuous activity. When murder is the outcome, many times it is committed by the child, who reacts with fatal violence to the abuser. It is commonly believed that parents who are involved in the sexual molestation of their children are of little physical threat to their children otherwise. Research conducted over the past several decades seems to validate these assumptions (see, e.g., Mohr, Turner, & Jerry, 1964; Revitch & Weiss, 1962; Righton, 1981; Virkunnen, 1981).

It is almost impossible for most parents to imagine harming their own children, let alone killing them. Clearly, however, some parents do kill their children. Only recently, for example, a young mother in Arkansas was arrested and charged with the murder of her infant daughter. An apparent believer in the occult, she had "burn sacrificed" her daughter so that the child's soul would become the property of the devil. She has entered a plea of not guilty (Charles Chastain, personal communication, May 10, 1992).

All women who kill are viewed very negatively in our society, of course, but mothers who kill their children are especially reviled. Perhaps because women are arrested for murder and manslaughter much less often than are men, when women are charged with such crimes, it seems to galvanize our attention. The recent celebrated murder cases involving Pamela Smart and Carolyn Warmus, for example, show that we are fascinated by women who kill. However, these cases, although they involve the killing of human beings, do not disturb us in the way that cases involving mothers who kill their own children disturb us.

Below, we present some of the research findings concerning parents who kill their children. Some studies have proposed particular social and psychological profiles that may be useful for mental health practitioners and criminal justice professionals who are working toward not only the apprehension of offenders but the early detection of possible offenders as well.

CHILDREN AS CHATTEL

Historically, children have been seen as chattel, that is, as the property of their parents, especially their fathers. In some societies, children are viewed as such until they reach "the age of reason." Upon reaching this magical age, the child is then supposed to act as an adult.

In some countries, families living under subsistence conditions practiced infanticide as one way to combat the economic problem of providing for children. To protect their ability to care for the already existing family members, parents (often mothers) who could not afford to care for another child would kill a new infant. The killing of females was especially prevalent because daughters were not viewed as being economic assets to the family. A daughter who was allowed to live was eventually married off, and her family paid a dowry of money, goods, or property to her new husband's family. The dowry was supposed to provide for the economic burden the groom would assume by taking a wife. In families that were especially poor or that had many daughters, female infanticide not only served to remove a pressing immediate problem but also eliminated the future need of a dowry (Whitehead & Lab, 1989, p. 41).

Families over the centuries have also resorted to many other means of dealing with children who present problems. At one time, abandonment, for example, had the same effect as the killing of a child. Children were sometimes sold into involuntary servitude or placed in apprenticeships away from home so they would not be a financial burden on the family. In other words, families have a long history of attempting to relieve themselves of unwanted or troublesome children. Financial strain has most often been at the center of these problems. Today, the stresses that lead to the murder of children have changed somewhat, but in some ways little has changed. As we show in the following sections, parents still sometimes kill the children they perceive as causing them problems.

MOTHERS WHO KILL

In a study examining homicides committed by women, D'Orban (1990) validated certain past assumptions concerning sex and murder. For example, murder was found to be almost exclusively a male action. Other studies, some of which will be mentioned later in this chapter, have estimated that almost three of four murders are perpetrated by males. In addition, D'Orban notes, women who kill have traditionally been labeled as mentally ill or suffering from other personal abnormalities. D'Orban found that in more than 80% of cases involving a female murderer, the woman has killed someone in her family. Almost 50% of the time, she has killed one of her children. Bourget and Bradford (1987) examined the professional literature and their own sample of parents who killed their children (the range of ages of the parents was 17 through 50, the children's age range was 0-12). They found that almost 7 of 10 perpetrators were mothers whose actions were triggered by psychosocial stresses, particularly some type of perceived social stress: abandonment by the husband or family, or the loss of economic resources for her own and her baby's survival.

There are definite risks to children, depending in no small part on the social stresses and unique social experiences to which the mother is exposed. Risk factors also include the child's age, birth order, and sex. The second author recently conducted an analysis of records in the state of Kentucky on mothers who murder their children; this analysis yields some interesting data. The results of this research are not unlike those of other studies that have been conducted on samples from other regions of the United States. We report the results of the Kentucky study in the following subsections. It should be kept in mind that murder is not regional; when it comes to children who are murdered by their mothers, we believe the following data are relevant for all areas.

Mother's Age and Risk to the Child

The younger the mother when she becomes pregnant, the greater the risk to the child. Conversely, the older the mother at the time of impregnation, the lower the risk to the child. The reasons for these particular findings seem self-evident. A young mother, especially a teenager, is less likely than a more mature mother to have the coping abilities needed to take care of an infant on her own, and may be less likely to have social support or family help. The pressures on a young mother can mount up and lead to despair.

Mother's Marital Status and Risk to the Child

The mother's marital status also appears to be a factor in a child's risk of homicide at the hands of the mother. In the Kentucky sample, more single mothers than married mothers had killed their children, and of the single mothers, divorced mothers killed less often than did never-married mothers. Mothers who are both single and young, who may have no sources of emotional or financial support, may be overwhelmed by the stresses of trying to rear a child alone.

Age of the Child and Risk of Homicide

The Kentucky data indicate that a child's risk of murder decreases once he or she reaches the age of 1 year. The age of greatest vulnerability appears to be in the first year of life. There is another peak of risk after the child grows into the teenage years, when the stresses and demands of parenthood go through many changes. These demands are different in nature and extent from those that appear to put the child at risk in infancy. It may be, in addition, that for some parents the value of the child increases as the child grows older. As children grow into adolescence, however, in general they come into greater conflict with their parents.

From the research conducted in Kentucky, it appears that murders involving older children are usually associated with maternal depression. This finding is supported by statements made by some of the mothers who killed their older children. Almost one-fourth of these women later killed themselves as well. Their suicides sometimes occurred almost immediately after the deaths of their children. This behavior is congruent with Durkheim's concept of anomie. Such a murder of a child is seen by the mother as an act of love. She feels the world is such a terrible place that she feels she must take not only her own life but also the life of her beloved offspring. The Kentucky records note one such case in which a young mother, age 35, shot and killed her 16-year-old daughter and then herself while they sat in a parked car at a public park. Her suicide note reflected her confusion and depression over the way she felt her life was crumbling. Because her life was in a state of chaos, she perceived that her daughter would suffer the same set of deplorable circumstances, and she could not bear to have her daughter experience that sorrow and despair.

Seldom does a mother kill more than one child in a murder/suicide. A mother who takes her child's life this way feels she is doing it out of love, as the documents left behind by such women have shown. This is not the case for the type of killers we call "family annihilators"; these are discussed in Chapter 5, which addresses mass murder. Such fathers who kill, like Ronald Simmons, George Banks, and Michael Perry, kill not only their children but adult family members as well.

Summary

The Kentucky data indicate that women who kill their children typically became pregnant very young, are single, have few financial or family resources, and are often depressed or suffer from great feelings of anomie. We have interviewed a number of women currently in prison for the murder of their children, and we have found this profile to be amazingly accurate. The case of one young woman we spoke with is frighteningly typical: Joanie (a pseudonym) is 21 years old and is currently serving a 25-year sentence in Kentucky for the murder of her son. Joanie's husband left her when she announced that she was pregnant. Her parents had adamantly opposed her marriage and had expelled Joanie from the family circle when she decided to marry her husband. Joanie encountered several financial and personal problems almost immediately after her husband left her, and after she had her baby she perceived herself to be utterly alone, with no one in the world who cared for her. She drowned her son and had entertained thoughts about ending her own life when she was apprehended by the local police.

FATHERS WHO KILL

There are, unfortunately, many examples of fathers who kill their sons and daughters. John List, who could also be classified as a family annihilator, killed his children and his wife. The same can be said of Ronald Eugene Simmons and of many other men (Marshall & Williams, 1991). The point here is that fathers who kill their children do so out of different motivations and expected gains from those experienced by mothers who kill. Mothers who kill their children tend to have particular personality traits that influence their actions. Fathers who kill their children do not necessarily demonstrate any of these traits.

Daly and Wilson (1988) found that fathers who kill are on the average four years older than mothers who kill. (This difference may simply be a function of the mean age differences in men and women who marry; that is, men tend to marry women who are slightly younger than them.) Daly and Wilson (1988) also found that fathers are more likely to kill older children. As mentioned above, mothers are more likely to kill infants, and children who reach the age of 1 are safer from their mothers than are younger children. Also, as in the cases of Simmons and List, a man will often kill not only one child but all of the children in the home, as well as his wife. Afterward, he may commit suicide. Daly and

Wilson report that 43% of fathers who kill older children commit suicide afterward; only 10% who kill infants then kill themselves.

Daly and Wilson also report that fathers are more likely to kill their sons and that mothers are more likely to kill their daughters. It may be that this same-sex bias reflects a form of competition within the family. This sense of competition transcends the family, especially for males. Males in general appear to have more difficulty than females in establishing relationships without an element of competition present on various levels (Bolton, Morris, & MacEachron, 1989; Knox, 1984).

Men are more likely to kill their entire families than are women. In a sample of Canadian male and female killers, no women were found who killed their spouses and children. This was not the case for men who killed (Daly & Wilson, 1988). Daly and Wilson report that in the period under consideration there were 61 episodes of men killing their spouses and their children; no cases of women committing such acts were found. "Familicide" appears to be a male crime.

From the above information it is apparent that fathers who kill their children are fundamentally different from mothers who kill their children. We now examine the murder of children by stepparents, an area that has for the most part been neglected in the professional literature.

STEPPARENTS WHO KILL

Traditional children's stories often depict stepparents, especially stepmothers, as evil. The "wicked stepmother" is a recurring figure in fairy tales, and stepparents in these stories are not viewed as having the maternal or paternal roles or feelings of biological parents. Real stepparents, of course, are not like those found in fairy tales; the vast majority love and care for their stepchildren as best they can, taking on true maternal and paternal feelings and duties. However, the ugly stepparents depicted by children's fiction are not too far from the truth in some cases.

Daly and Wilson (1988) report that in almost 15% of the known cases of physical child abuse, stepparents are the abusers. Of course, it must be remembered that these data come only from reported cases. Daly and Wilson estimate that children who are in homes with stepparents are *100 times more likely* to be fatally abused than are children who live with both their biological parents.

Especially disturbing are those cases in which stepfathers physically and/or sexually abuse and even end up killing their stepchildren while the biological mothers attempt to deny the existence of the abuse. Such mothers may feel they need to weigh the risks involved to themselves also, and may feel forced to choose between their children and their mates. Obviously, women who are in this situation have very difficult choices to make; it seems that too often they may look the other way while their children are being not only physically abused but murdered.

As is the case with a child's risk of murder by a natural parent, the risk of murder by a stepparent, especially the stepfather, appears to be influenced by the child's age. Data we gathered from the Crimes Against Children Unit in Louisville, Kentucky, show a direct relationship. Very young children—that is, under the age of 2—are at greater risk. The risk then drops steadily to about the age of 7, and then slowly rises again until the child reaches the age of majority, although the risk is never again as high as it is in infanthood. How this unpublished research compares with other studies and empirical research is unknown at this time. Clearly, more research needs to be done in this area.

CONCLUSION

It is very difficult for most people to understand those who fatally abuse children. Westley Dodd, the serial killer discussed earlier in this chapter, said in a 1991 interview on the television program *48 Hours* that he himself could not understand how he could "love children so much" and yet do the things he did to his child victims. Like many others who attack and kill children, Dodd made the connection between fatal violence and sexual gratification. There is no easy explanation for how this connection begins. Perhaps mysopeds are indeed psychopaths with no feelings of empathy, remorse, or social conscience whatsoever. Psychopathy is not a rare personality disorder; we have seen this ourselves in our many interviews with sex offenders and murderers in prison. When one researcher interviewed Ted Bundy,

Randy Woodfield, Douglas Clark, and others after they were imprisoned, he noted their "cardboard" personalities—there was a lack of affect in their descriptions of their deeds. Dr. Al Carlisle, psychologist at Utah State Prison, who has also interviewed "celebrated" killers such as Arthur Bishop and Ted Bundy, has noted the same phenomenon (personal communication, March 28, 1991).

In society's attempts to deal with the problems of child abuse and murder, national telephone hot lines have been established. Maybe taking such steps is one way in which we as citizens can believe we are really doing something about this problem. Pictures of missing children appear on milk cartons, on the backs of trucks, on billboards, and on television. Does this all make us feel better? Probably yes. Does it do anything at all to increase our understanding of the problem of the sadistic pedophile? Obviously, no. What can be done? Better education is one step. People in general need to realize that it is very difficult to change someone who prefers children as sexual partners and murder as the capstone of the relationship. But national hysteria is not the answer.

Even more difficult to understand is the parent who fatally injures his or her own child. The family is supposed to be a place of warmth, safety, comfort, and acceptance, but this is clearly not always the case. The family has become for many a "cradle of violence" where the child is in imminent danger of becoming a murder statistic. As noted above, mothers who kill their children are certainly different from fathers who kill, but knowing about these differences alone does little to help us understand the personality of the killer parent. We can enumerate certain personality traits—anomie, depression, alcoholism, and so on—but what we need is a better understanding of the total personality of the parent who kills and the stresses that can result in the murder of a child. Most parents have at one time or another found themselves in situations where they have felt the urge to "knock their children's heads off." Why do some stop short of harming their children and others act out their anger and brutalize or even kill their children? We need further empirical research and the translation of the results of that research into counseling and rehabilitation techniques that are effective with parents who have the potential to kill.

4

Hate Groups and Homicide

Perhaps the darkest period that can come in any nation's history is when a group of overtly or covertly united organizations emerge with a manifest purpose of exercising violence against an out-group.[1] The group selected for victimization is often characterized by a theological belief system, skin color, age, ethnic background, or sexual orientation. Many such groups are currently operating covertly in North America: the Ku Klux Klan (KKK), the Identity church, Skinheads, and others. The Anti-Defamation League of B'nai B'rith estimates that there are as many as 71 groups currently operating in the United States. These groups are responsible for untold numbers of acts of violence and homicides motivated by hate (Mickolus, Sandler, & Murdock, 1989; Sterling, 1981; Stohl, 1988). The violent homicidal acts perpetrated by hate groups are directed toward their "enemies." Many victims of this violence, however, such as those in law enforcement, may simply happen to come into contact with the groups at the time of the violence.

This chapter discusses several hate groups, describing their members and ideologies. We examine these groups' various philosophical positions and the unique problems each group presents. Although the hate groups described in this chapter are all somewhat different, they all share a common thread of ideology: Each group is made up of members who consider

themselves to be "the chosen people" and who consider their
prescribed role to be that of eradicating "undesirables." The
manner in which they go about doing so is often very violent.

THE KU KLUX KLAN

Americans are all too familiar with the gross violence committed by the KKK: cross burnings, lynchings of scores of minorities, and other atrocities. The Klan is the longest-lived extremist group in the United States (White, 1991, p. 25). At the
height of its terror, from 1870 to 1903, at least 1,985 blacks were
hanged or burned alive by the Ku Klux Klan and other southern
lynch mobs (Brown, 1979, p. 31). By 1870, the membership of
the Klan had risen to almost 600,000. During the latter stages of
the nineteenth century, the killings occurred most often in
Florida, Alabama, Georgia, and Louisiana.

In the early 1960s, three young civil rights workers, James
Chaney, Andrew Goodman, and Michael Schwerner, were murdered by Klan members in Mississippi. In July 1965, a black man,
Lieutenant Colonel Lemuel Penn, was killed by shots from a passing
car in Athens, Georgia. In 1965, Violoa Gregg Liuzzo, a white civil
rights worker, was murdered by three Klansmen. In 1966, this time
in Mississippi, Vernon Dahmer, an NAACP official, died of burns
he received when his house was firebombed by the Klan.

In the 1980s in Florida, Maryland, Tennessee, Kentucky,
North Carolina, Georgia, Alabama, New York, and Ohio, violent
cases of Klan activities were chronicled in the courts. These
illegal activities, justified in the minds of the perpetrators by a
theology of racism and ethnicity, involved cross burnings, trans-
porting firearms across state lines, shootings, assaults, and other
sundry incidents of violence.

The Klan's agenda of violence is reinforced by a belief system
based on "white supremacy." This doctrine has guided the
group's violence since its inception.

History of the Klan

The KKK was founded on Christmas Eve in 1865 in Pulaski,
Tennessee, by six Confederate soldiers. They derived the name

of their organization from the Greek word *kuklos,* which means circle. Originally only a fraternal group, the circle later began to undertake acts of violence intended to maintain the white race's superior position. The fundamental objective of the KKK since its inception has been "the maintenance of the White Race in their Republic by terror and intimidation" (Kirkham, Levy, & Crofty, 1970, p. 216). Soon the assaults and murders of non-whites started.

Disguised in white robes and hoods with masks, members of the KKK roamed the countryside to terrorize their "enemies" and commit acts of violence that often resulted in murder. In 1867, the U.S. Congress passed the Reconstruction Act, which substituted military governments for the local government units. Four years later, Congress passed the Ku Klux Klan Act and the Force Act, outlawing the Klan and forcing it to operate in a clandestine fashion. Believing their power was being eroded, Klan leaders dedicated themselves to the restoration of power to whites. They adopted a platform that included promises of aid to widows and children, relief of the injured and oppressed, and the protection of the weak and helpless (as long as they were not black).

The history of the Klan can be divided into three stages. The first stage began with the end of the Civil War and the founding of the KKK. The end of slavery and the postwar Reconstruction created a fertile time for the development of an organization predicated upon hate and the exercise of violence. The Klan's major goal at this time was to fight what it saw as federal interference in southern affairs. This goal appeared to have been achieved when white Southern Democrats again won power in government (Vetter & Perlstein, 1991, p. 43), and, having fulfilled its perceived mission, the Klan voluntarily disbanded. As Gurr (1988) notes, the white-dominated social order was then continued "peaceably and legally through the segregationist policies of state and local government and violently by lynching mobs" (p. 554).

The second stage of the KKK began on Thanksgiving night, 1915, in Stone Mountain, Georgia. The leader and initiator was William Joseph Simmons. This time, the KKK focused upon a message of hate and violence directed toward a much broader base of minorities, this time including those with certain memberships in religion, such as Catholics and Jews. Blacks soon became a secondary target for the activities of the Klan. According

Klan Terminology

AKIA	a password (stands for "a Klansman, I am")
alien	non-Klansman
AYAK	a password (stands for "Are you a Klansman?")
banished	expelled from membership in the Klan
citizen of the Invisible Empire	a Klan member
exalted cyclops	head of a klavern (chapter president)
grand dragon	head of a realm (usually a state)
imperial wizard	chief of the Invisible Empire, national leader
Invisible Empire	the universal geographic jurisdiction of a Klan
ITSUB	a correspondence sign-off (stands for "In the sacred unfailing bond")
KBI	the Klan Bureau of Investigation; checks for leaks and obtains information about the "enemy"
KIGY	a password (stands for "Klansman, I greet you")
klabee	treasurer
kladd	conductor of naturalization ceremony
klaliff	vice president
Klan symbols	sword, water, robe and hood, American flag, cross, and the Bible, King James version, open to 12 Romans (symbols are required to be placed on altar at klavern meetings)
Klankraft	practices and beliefs of the Klan
klarogo	inner guard/security
klavern	local chapter
kleagle	organizer
klectoken	initiation fee
klexter	outer guard/security
kligrapp	secretary
klokan	three-man investigating committee, composed of the nighthawk, klarogo, and klexter
klokard	lecturer
klonsel	grand attorney (national title)
Kloran	book used to conduct Klan ceremonies
kludd	chaplain
Konstitution	rules and bylaws
myok	Klan emblem
naturalization	induction into membership
nighthawk	keeper of property of the klavern; in charge of security
passport	Klan membership card
province	congressional district
realm	state organization
SANBOG	a password (stands for "Strangers are near, be on guard")
SOR	sign of recognition
titan	head of a province (usually a congressional district)
wreck	action taken by a wrecking crew against a person
wrecking crew or action squad	five to eight members who are charged with taking physical action against wayward members or enemies of the Klan; headed by a nighthawk; conduct own private meetings, separate from klavern; receive orders from exalted cyclops of klavern; actions must also be approved by kludd

SOURCE: Anti-Defamation League of B'nai B'rith, Civil Rights Division (1988, pp. 87-88).

to Weiner et al. (1990), Klan violence often was actually directed more toward the "ne'er-do-wells, and the allegedly immoral of the very same background as the Klansmen: white, Anglo-Saxon Protestant" (p. 12). This stage passed in the 1920s largely because of general public disapproval of the violence perpetrated by members of the KKK. This disgust with violence, coupled with political, bribery, and other scandals involving the national leaders of the KKK (one leader was "arrested not quite fully clothed in a police raid in a bawdy house"; Bullard, 1991, p. 15), led to its eventual decline (Chalmers, 1965).

The third stage of the Klan commenced shortly after World War II, and this time the group's energies and activities were directed toward fighting civil rights and desegregation. With the Supreme Court's decision in *Brown v. Board of Education,* the KKK launched a campaign that included murders, cross burnings, and beatings of civil rights workers. The federal government was given the charge of law enforcement duties dealing with these crimes (Vetter & Perlstein, 1991, p. 57). Into the 1950s and 1960s, Klan-perpetrated brutality was a common occurrence. For example, in 1957, a black man, Judge Aaron, was abducted by the Klan in Alabama. They castrated him and poured turpentine over his wounds.

Despite the best efforts of local and federal law enforcement agencies, the Klan is still in operation. The organization's activities are more clandestine at some times than at others. Witness the violence that erupted in Forsyth County, Georgia, in 1987, when what started as a peaceful march in honor of Martin Luther King, Jr.'s birthday was disrupted by Klansmen and soon became a full-blown riot (Anti-Defamation League of B'nai B'rith, Civil Rights Division, 1987b).

Klan Membership

The exact number of members of the modern Klan is unknown. From a peak membership of almost 60,000 immediately following World War II, the numbers have greatly decreased. Federal intelligence operations indicate that the numbers fluctuate depending on membership interest, which can be influenced by contemporary social concerns.

Estimated Klan Membership	
1871	550,000
1920	5,000
1925	5,000,000
1927	350,000
1965	42,000
1974	1,500
1978	9,000
1981	11,000
1990	5,000

SOURCE: Bullard (1991).

Within the larger national Klan, there are several Klan groups throughout the United States, including the following:

- United Klans of America
- Invisible Empire, Knights of the Ku Klux Klan
- Knights of the Ku Klux Klan (Tuscumbia faction)
- Knights of the Ku Klux Klan (Don Black faction)
- Southern National Front
- Christian Knights of the Ku Klux Klan

Other components unaffiliated with the national organization include the Florida White Knights, Ohio Knights, Independent Order of Knights (Maryland), New Order Knights (Missouri), Invisible Empire Knights (New Jersey), White Unity Party (Pennsylvania), American Knights (California), Knights of the White Camelia (Texas), and Southern White Knights (Georgia).

The largest segment of the KKK, the United Klans of America, was headed by Imperial Wizard Robert Shelton in the 1960s. It is a predominantly southern organization, with klaverns in Alabama, Florida, Indiana, Kentucky, North Carolina, South Carolina, and Virginia. It publishes a newsletter titled *The Fiery Cross*.

Members of the United Klans of America have been arrested and tried for terrorist acts and murder. In 1981, for example, member James Knowles was convicted for the murder of Michael Donald. In 1985, five members of this group were charged

---

Klan Anti-Semitism Message

Excerpt from a recorded telephone message of the Invisible Empire in Pensacola, Florida:

Listen Whitey, the Jews have taken over America and you are too damn ignorant to see it. They are pouring out your tax money to the niggers and you are too damn brainwashed to know it. The Jews are pouring out pro-nigger, pro-Jew poison to you over the Jew-owned TV and you are so damn stupid that you swallow it. The Christ-killing Jew has seized the reins of government and passed laws to imprison you if you raise your hand against the nigger, and you don't have the brains to do a damn thing about it. . . . He has filled your schools with stinkin' niggers and you have taken it laying down. You are now reaping your reward . . . you no longer have what it takes to hunt down the white-hating instigators who are destroying you.

SOURCE: Anti-Defamation League of B'nai B'rith, Civil Rights Division (1988, p. 18).

---

with planning terrorist acts against minorities and with conducting training to carry out those acts. In 1986, they were found guilty of violating Florida's paramilitary training statute. In attempting to cause social turmoil, these men developed strategies designed to incite blacks to riot so that more whites would join the KKK.

The Knights of the Ku Klux Klan (KKKK) was founded by David Duke in the 1970s. Membership fluctuated during that time, in no small part because of a great deal of discord within the group. Duke was replaced by Bill Wilkinson in 1979. Under his leadership, the KKKK took a pseudomilitary stance, insisting upon militaristic training and direct confrontation. In 1979, Wilkinson and others were involved in a confrontation with blacks who were protesting the conviction of a severely retarded black man accused of raping a white woman. Two blacks were shot in the head and one Klansman was shot in the chest, another in the leg.

By 1982, the power and membership of the Klan had greatly diminished. Wilkinson received a great deal of negative publicity when he was accused of being an FBI informant and of arranging for clandestine infiltration of agents into the KKKK. He denied these allegations and said that whatever information the FBI received could have been obtained through local and national newspapers. Wilkinson was eventually replaced by James Farrands in 1986. A Roman Catholic and a tool and die maker, Farrands led the KKK despite other leaders' vying for the grand wizardry, such as Tom Metzger in California and Tom Black in Alabama (Anti-Defamation League of B'nai B'rith, Civil Rights Division, 1987b, pp. 3-39; Bullard, 1991, pp. 56-57).

Without a strong national structure to provide leadership and plans for their crimes of violence, splinter groups have formed under the leadership of varied personalities who view violence as a utilitarian act. These groups are led by diverse leaders with varying ideologies. When certain social concerns come to the forefront of the consciousness of persons disposed to violent action, these splinter groups form and Klan membership increases. For example, the issue of segregation led to a great influx of new members into the Klan. The temporary rise in Klan membership in the 1970s may have been influenced by the battles waged to challenge court-ordered busing of schoolchildren, equal opportunity in the workplace, and immigration policies and actions.

There may currently be a downward trend in Klan membership, but there are still indications that various organizations are in operation whose manifest purpose is to instill terror through the commission of violent acts, including murder (Brown, 1979; Lieberman, 1991; Weiner et al., 1990). Cohler (1989) and Magnuson (1989) both report that an anti-Semitic newspaper distributed through the office of David Duke has 30,000 subscribers. Regardless of the exact membership of groups like the KKK, those involved are share a mind-set of violence.

THE IDENTITY CHURCH

Some of the many organizations adopting a philosophy of white supremacy are part of a movement known as the Identity church. Based upon bigotry supported by a perverse religious dogma, those who share this "theology" believe that whites are the true "chosen people of God." They believe that whites are naturally superior to all other races, and they place all nonwhites in a category with animals. Identity church members especially despise Jews; they see Jews as the main enemy because they believe that Jews control the "white man's" destiny through economic sanctions and strongholds.

Many of the believers in the Identity church hold that the second coming of Jesus Christ is imminent. Like Charles Manson and his followers, they believe that the second coming will be preceded by a monumental race war followed by a Communist attack upon the United States. The only survivors of this two-pronged invasion will be the members of the Identity church.

The Ideology of Hate:
The Theology of the Identity Movement

Several groups make up the Identity church. These groups have ideological commonalities, such as a belief in the superiority of the white race and the belief that whites are the chosen people, but each group has its own leader and is headquartered in a different part of the United States.

The roots of the Identity church lie in mid-nineteenth-century England. The theology preaches a literal interpretation of the King James version of the Bible. Because whites are believed to be the true chosen people, it follows that England and the new American colonies *must* indeed be the chosen land, the Israel promised in the Bible itself. An interesting dichotomy has developed from this interpretation. Whites accrue all the benefits of the chosen ones. All curses and ills are the inheritance of Judah, represented by modern-day Jews. Moreover, Jesus was not a Jew, according to Identity doctrine; He was of Israel, not Judah. Jesus, then, is the "father" of the whites who later inhabited England, Germany, and Scandinavia. All whites then become, de facto, the chosen people.

The most famous of the early Identity "church fathers" is Dr. Wesley Swift. Soon after World War II, this one-time Ku Klux Klan organizer founded the Christian Defense League, and he later became the leader of the Anglo-Saxon Christian Congregation in Los Angeles. Swift, anti-Semitic and anti-Catholic, was a colleague of Gerald L. K. Smith, another racist and anti-Semite who led the Christian Nationalist Crusade. He also published an inflammatory journal, *The Cross and the Flag.* He promised that by 1950 no Jew would be alive in the United States.

Swift died in 1970. The leadership passed to the Reverend Richard Butler, leader of an Idaho-based hate group called the Aryan Nation. Butler's church, the Church of Jesus Christ Christian, advocated hatred and violence against Jews and other selected targets. All of the smaller organizations within the Identity church movement, including those calling themselves churches, are devoted to spreading hate and committing violence in the name of their "religious" beliefs.

Identity Church Organizations

There are multiple churches professing the hate theology. These churches vary only slightly in ideology; the crucial differences among them rest with their founding personalities and their current leadership. The groups are scattered across the United States, but most are found in the South.

Aryan Nation. The Aryan Nation is headquartered in Hayden Lake, Idaho. Founded upon the principles of Butler's Church of Jesus Christ Christian, the group is devoted to the original principles of Wesley Swift. It is similar to Nazism in its approach: the dogma, ritual, and material trappings. Its philosophy concerning blacks and Jews is blatantly bigoted and violent. The insignia of the organization includes a swastika, a symbol of its mission to "eradicate undesirables."

For the past 10 years the members of the Aryan Nation have convened an annual Aryan Nation Congress. Attended by racists and white supremacists, these conferences have featured speakers from the Mountain Church of Jesus Christ, the KKK, and other right-wing organizations. Criminal activity and violence have been integral parts of the Aryan Nation's practice since its founding. However, according to White (1991), who states that there are fortunately fewer than 5,000 members in the Aryan Nation, only a few dozen members support the doctrine of violence (p. 23).

Recently, Butler was arrested and charged with conspiracy to overthrow the government of the United States; he was found not guilty.

Christian Defense League. This group, led by James Warner, is based in Baton Rouge and Arabi, Louisiana. It claims to be the one true voice of the white people and advocates violence as the sole means of eradicating the "Jew problem."

The Christian Defense League is closely related to the New Christian Crusade Church, also founded by Warner in 1971, based in Metairie, Louisiana. The members have published materials with such titles as *New Research Into Jewish Ritual Murder, American Jews Are Khazars,* and *Inequalities of the Negro Race,* all basically emotional tirades against blacks and Jews.

Posse Comitatus. The Posse Comitatus takes its name from the Latin for "power of the county." Active since 1969, the group is made up of loosely organized cells (in California, Colorado, Delaware, Idaho, Illinois, Kansas, Michigan, Nebraska, North Dakota, Oregon, Texas, Washington, and Wisconsin) committed to the idea that the federal government is the enemy and that the law should rest within the individual's county of residence. Members believe that God condones their violence and that Jews are in control of the country's financial destiny, and they are bent upon using violence to solve the "Jew problem" and return governing power to the local level. Some members refuse to pay taxes even to the point of imprisonment as a nonviolent ploy to disrupt government functioning.

Violent acts, including homicide, have been attributed to the Posse since its inception, and such violence has been well documented. For example, in 1983 member Gordon Kahl, along with several other members, killed two U.S. marshals. Kahl was hunted for months before he was killed by federal agents in Arkansas (Corcoran, 1991).

The Covenant, the Sword, and the Arm of the Lord. This organization, also known as the CSA, maintains a paramilitary support system intent on violence. Believing that the country is edging toward economic collapse, the CSA trains members to assume their place in the new society. Located in Arkansas and Missouri, the CSA promotes a philosophy of hate, racism, and anti-Semitism.

One high-ranking CSA official believes that God has spoken to him personally. In this apparition, God commanded the CSA to conduct seminars in military preparedness for the trial to come. Intelligence reports on this group indicate that members have taught seminars devoted to urban warfare, riflery and pistol craft, and military tactics, and have sold riot weapons. Prolific CSA writers have published materials with such titles as *Protocols of the Elders of Zion, The Talmud Unmasked, Who's Who in the Zionist Conspiracy, The Negro and the World Crisis,* and *A Straight Look at the Third Reich.*

The CSA was disbanded only recently, and its members have moved to the other right-wing groups.

The Christian Patriot Defense League. The Christian Patriot Defense League (CPDL) is a right-wing extremist survivalist group heavily involved in paramilitary training and education. The group preaches against the ideology of Communism and predicts the imminent demise of the United States. Members are in a constant state of military preparedness.

The leaders of CPDL preach a message of returning to what they interpret to be basic Christian principles. They advocate military preparedness against the Antichrist, no doubt a Communist. This organization is affiliated with other known paramilitary groups, such as the Citizens Emergency Defense System and the Paul Revere Club (a fund-raising operation).

Headquartered at one time in Louisville, Illinois, the CPDL takes as its mission the awakening of patriots to what it believes are very real dangers threatening the lives of all Americans. Members have published materials with such titles as *The Negro: A Beast, The Origins of the Jews,* and *National Vanguard.* They preach violence against certain minorities and the supremacy of the white race.

The Order. The Order, or the Silent Brotherhood, is an underground terrorist group that is part of the Aryan Nation confederacy. Alternately called the White American Bastion and the Aryan Resistance Movement, this group, which originated from members of the Aryan Nation and the CSA, has launched a campaign of violence since its inception in 1983. Many of the group's members have been recruited while in prison.

A major goal of the Order is to overthrow the U.S. government, which is judged to be pro-Judah. In fact, the organization's literature refers to the U.S. government as the Zionist Occupation Government, or ZOG. In their materials they threaten to hang members of Congress and kill other members of government, including federal agents and other "combatants" in the group's holy war: local police, journalists, bankers, judges, and business leaders.

Many of the more violent members of the Order have already been arrested and convicted for violent crimes against society. For example, in 1985, nine men and one woman were sent to prison for sentences ranging from 40 years to life for various criminal acts and civil rights violations. In that same year, David Tate, a member of the Order, was convicted of the slaying of a state trooper in Missouri and given a life sentence. Perhaps one of the Order's most infamous acts was the assassination of radio talk show host Alan Berg in Denver. Richard Scutari, one of the FBI's 10 most wanted, although acquitted in the Berg case, was given a 60-year prison sentence on charges of racketeering and conspiracy connected with the robbery of a multimillion-dollar Brink's armored car robbery in 1984 in Utah. In 1986, Eldon Cutler was convicted of paying an undercover FBI agent $2,000 to decapitate a government informant. He was sentenced to 12 years in prison. In 1988, two members were arrested for allegedly planning to kill Jesse Jackson, who was seeking his party's presidential nomination at the time (White, 1991, p. 27).

A blatant goal of the Order is to kill all Jews. The Jews, according to the Order's gospel, are responsible for all social and economic ills, and the only way to get rid of these ills is to eliminate the source.

The Order's beliefs incorporate elements of Norse mythology and personal immortality, and their language and behavior often contain Nordic references. According to White (1991), for example, when Order members executed a government informant, they spoke of striking him in the back of the head with "the hammer of Thor" (p. 27).

The Committee of the States. This organization, also known as the Committee of the States in Congress Assembled, first came to national attention in 1985 because of an article that appeared in the *Daily Journal* in Los Angeles. Founded in 1984, it is similar in its beliefs to the Posse Comitatus.

Because of the great possibility that the Committee of the States will foment violence based in right-wing patriotism, the group's members have been under investigation by federal law enforcement agencies. Several high-ranking members of this group, including William Gale, Richard Van Hazel, and George McCray, have been outspoken in advocating violence (Anti-Defamation League of B'nai B'rith, Civil Rights Division, 1988, p. 45).

SKINHEADS

Besides the groups described above, there are yet other splinter groups that propagate similar messages of hate and violence. All of these groups are a great danger to all nonwhites as well as others who may be in sympathy with targeted groups, such as homosexuals, Jews, and Catholics. Many of the young people who have moved into these hate groups are known as Skinheads.

Skinheads are not unique to North America; the movement originated in England in the late 1960s. British Skinheads were mainly working-class youth reacting to British immigration policies regarding West Indians and Pakistanis. These immigrants were thought to be taking jobs away from English natives. Skinhead behavior grew quite violent; it often came in the form of beatings and other physical attacks, including murder.

With an ideology based on violence, Skinheads were reacting to those they viewed as liberal, middle-class, and "sissified." The movement caught hold and quickly spread to other countries, including West Germany, France, Belgium, and Sweden. Even in East Germany (which was Communist at the time), a group of Skinheads was sent to prison for desecration of a Jewish cemetery.

Skinheads in the United States

In the late 1970s, the Skinhead movement spread to the United States; many young people were originally attracted to the movement by the music of Skinhead bands, mostly British. The message of this music, and of the movement, is clear: hatred, violence, even murder.

Skinhead Terminology

bashing	attacks on members of "enemy" groups, such as gays, Jews, blacks, Asians, and other minorities
boot boys	Skinheads who perpetrate violence on others (violence often takes the form of kicking with boots)
braces	suspenders; worn as part of the Skinhead uniform
crop	the close-shaved hairstyle of Skinheads
Dr. Martens	black English work boots with steel toes, typically worn with white laces; worn as part of the Skinhead uniform
Fred Perrys	tennis shirts, always worn with the top button fastened (optional part of the uniform)
headbanging	a form of dancing popular with Skinheads (typified by dancers bumping into each other, usually danced to rock and roll music)
jump in	initiation rite in which a new member jumps into the middle of a group and is beaten
networking	bringing several groups together in a common site so new information can be shared
oi	cockney for "hey," a form of music favored by Skinheads
regular night out	a "battle cry" used when attacking enemies
toll tax	money demanded in extortion; payment permits passage of the person into certain areas without the danger of being harmed

SOURCE: Adapted from lecture at Southern Police Institute, March 1993.

Often supervised by adults affiliated with Identity church organizations, Skinheads are taught early the message of violence. Tom Metzger and Richard Butler are but two of the leaders alleged to have organized the Skinhead movement in the United States. Metzger's son, John, is active in this movement. John received a great deal of publicity when he was on Geraldo Rivera's television talk show and a fight erupted between some members of the panel and the audience. Even the host of the show was involved in the melee; Rivera was hit in the nose with a chair.

The U.S. Marshals Service calls the Skinhead movement the most dangerous of contemporary movements in racism (U.S. Department of Justice, U.S. Marshals Service, 1989). Members wear uniforms that incorporate neo-Nazi insignia, and they preach violence against Jews, blacks, and other minorities. It is certain that the organization is active in many parts of North America.

Skinhead Philosophy

The philosophy of the Skinheads is little different from that of the Klan or Identity church organizations. Professing a hatred of minorities, especially Jews and blacks, the movement is geared toward the establishment of a complete white power structure in government, religion, and business. In recent years, Skinheads have added homosexuals, Hispanics, Asians, and other minorities to their list of hated others.

Like Identity church followers, Skinheads believe they are the direct descendants of the lost tribes of Israel and that England and the original American colonies are the true Israel. Therefore, it follows that Anglo-Saxons, not Jews, are the chosen people. The Jews are the children of Satan. In a quantum leap of theological rhetoric, blacks and other nonwhites are called "mud people" and are considered to be on the same level as animals. These mud people are considered to have no souls. In part because of this "religious" belief, there are continual violent confrontations between the Skinheads and their target groups.

Also like members of the Identity church, Skinheads believe the end of the world is near. They believe that U.S. cities will be destroyed by Communist attack and that an unavoidable race war will follow. Following this race war, the Skinheads believe, they and others who believe as they do will be the only ones to survive. Many Skinheads actually look forward to this Armageddon because of their theology.

Interestingly, Skinheads in general profess great patriotism and try to remain bodily "pure." Most do not believe in alcohol consumption and view drug use as not only physically harmful but against their basic theological principles.

Skinhead Violence

The Skinhead philosophy promotes acts of violence against all those who fit the category of "undesirables." For example, in one incident in a suburb of Los Angeles, a small group of Skinheads attacked an Iranian couple with a child. Beginning with verbal abuse, the youths finally physically assaulted the family. One black bystander came to their aid before the police arrived at the scene. The Skinheads were arrested in this incident. In 1987, a Skinhead was arrested in Los Angeles for the attempted murder of a young Hispanic woman. He slit her throat, but, fortunately, she survived the attack. A California group calling itself the American Front Skinheads has continually been involved with the criminal justice system for its violent attacks on Jews. Other groups include the Reich Skins, who at one time were suspected in the death of a musician in San Jose, California, and also of threatening to lynch a young black woman.

Skinhead crimes of violence are not limited to California. In Miami, Florida, for example, a police officer was stabbed in 1987 during a confrontation with Skinheads. In Orlando and Tampa, Skinhead demonstrations resulted in violence, and in 1987 two Skinheads were arrested and charged with the fatal stabbing of a black man in Tampa.

In Detroit, two Skinheads were found guilty in the murder of a young black woman. In Denver, a young Skinhead was charged in May 1989 with first-degree murder, kidnapping, arson, and aggravated robbery in the death of a hairdresser. In Salt Lake City, a young man was stomped to death by Skinheads. In Portland, Oregon, according to the medical examiner, there have been more than 50 such attacks, including the murder of an African man beaten to death with a baseball bat (Larry Lewmon, M.D., personal communication, June 30, 1992).

In Mobile, Alabama, two Skinheads decided to kill a black man. They abducted Michael Donald, a teenager walking to a local grocery store from his home, and murdered him. They hung his body from a tree so that other hate-group members could see what they had done. One of the murderers was sentenced to life in prison for this crime; the other was sentenced to death. Between 1987 and 1990, Skinheads were charged with at least a dozen murders (Bullard, 1991, p. 48).

Clearly, Skinheads have been active all over the United States. Their acts are well planned and often ensure their success. The bashing of gays, blacks, Jews, and others is the Skinheads' way of acting out their "theology." They wear heavy boots to stomp their victims into submission and even death, and it is not unusual for them to carry other weapons, including knives, guns, swagger sticks, baseball bats, and chains.

CONCLUSION

There are many more hate groups that have not been covered in this chapter, such as the Black Liberation Army, the Macheteros, the New World Liberation Front, Omega 7, United Freedom Front, and the Weather Underground. These and others like them are discussed in Chapter 7, which addresses terrorism and homicide. These groups are distinguished from the hate groups discussed in this chapter by their fundamental differences in philosophies, motivations, and anticipated gains.

Hate crimes in general appear to be on the increase in North America, especially crimes against gays and lesbians (Herek & Berrill, 1992). How much of this increase can be attributed to organized hate groups is not clear, but the youths involved in the Skinhead movement certainly are emerging as a threat, not only to their targeted victims but to society as a whole. Many of the hate groups discussed above have begun to form informational and membership links and to coordinate violent activities, and these may be beginning signs of national organization. If decisive action is not taken, further murders will most certainly occur. Because of the nature of hate groups, and the fact that their motivations are tied in with patriotism and "religious" beliefs, it is very difficult for authorities in mainstream society to establish a meaningful dialogue with them. There are no discernible signs of any gross reduction in membership or activity in these groups; given the current trends, it appears that murders and assaults are likely not only to continue but to increase.

NOTE

1. A great deal of the material presented in this chapter comes from publications of the U.S. Department of Justice, U.S. Marshals Service (1989) and from publications of the Anti-Defamation League of B'nai B'rith, Civil Rights Division (1983, 1987a, 1987b, 1987c, 1988, 1989).

5

Mass Murder

There is a great deal of misunderstanding about what is meant by the term *mass murder*. Often the terms *mass murder, serial murder,* and *spree murder* are used interchangeably, even though there are fundamental differences among these three forms of multicide (i.e., the killing of three or more victims). Each of these three types of murder involves unique motivations, anticipated gains, methods of victim selection, methods of killing, and other important elements.

This chapter examines only one form of multicide, mass murder. Within this type of murder, some elements will differ. For example, the weapon used may be a gun, arson, or a bomb smuggled aboard an airplane. The anticipated gains of mass murderers may vary also. This chapter explores the nature of mass murder in depth, and points out the ways in which it is distinct from serial and spree murder.

WHAT IS MASS MURDER?

Simply stated, mass murder is the killing of a number of persons at one time and in one place. Obviously, however, there is more to mass murder than this simple definition. It is immediately

71

apparent that there are elements that separate mass murder from other forms of homicide.

The preceding definition is a useful starting point for differentiating mass murder from other forms of multicide. One issue to be decided is how many people are considered "a number." How many people need to die in order for a mass murder to be considered to have taken place? Holmes and De Burger (1985, 1988) and Hickey (1991) suggest that three is the appropriate number. Other researchers, such as Hazelwood and Douglas (1980), believe that four deaths should be the criterion. Dietz (1986) offers the number of three as the critical mass of victims for a case to be called mass murder, "if we define mass murder as the wilful injuring of five or more persons of whom three of more are killed by a single offender in a single incident" (p. 480).

Dietz's definition is cumbersome, especially because it adds the element of injured victims to the basic definition. Of course, if only 2 persons are killed and 30 are saved through heroic actions taken by medical personnel, would this not be a mass murder situation? Such are the games played by anyone who tries to use only a base number as an integral part of a definition. We prefer to consider three the critical number, without consideration of others who may be injured and would have died if not for emergency and successful medical care. The critical concern in the definition is the number of persons who are murdered.

Time and place are two further elements in the basic definition of mass murder. The above definition specifies that the murders must occur "at one time and in one place." Typically the act of mass murder is carried out in a single episodic act of violence. An example is the 1984 incident that took place at a McDonald's restaurant in San Ysidro, California. The victims, 40 in all (21 died), just happened to be together in one place, the restaurant, and the killings all occurred over a very short time span. However, it is prudent to recognize that mass murders may be carried out over a longer period, say, minutes or even a few hours apart, and also at more than one geographic location, perhaps only a few blocks apart. For example, a mass killer may go into one business establishment and kill several customers and then go across town and kill another person. This may be considered an act of mass murder despite the fact that it did not occur strictly "at one time and in one place."

In summary, the definition of mass murder has four components:

- the number of victims
- the location of the murders
- the time period in which the killings are carried out
- the distance from one murder site to another

These components illustrate the important differences among mass murder, serial murder, and spree murder. Serial murder is defined as the killing of three or more persons with more than a 30-day period transpiring between the first and the last kills. Spree murder is the killing of three or more persons usually within a 30-day period. With spree murder, there is typically an accompanying commission of a felony, such as robbery. The determination of the form of a multicide is the first step toward a successful resolution of the case; this determination holds the key to an understanding of the character of the person who would commit such an act.

Other Significant Differences

One additional difference between mass murder and serial murder is that mass murderers often die at the scenes of their crimes, either by committing suicide or by placing themselves in a situation where they "force" the police to take lethal action. In only a few cases do they turn themselves in to the police after their deeds are done. Serial killers, on the other hand, take great pains to avoid detection and take elaborate measures to elude apprehension (Hickey, 1991; Holmes & De Burger, 1985, 1988).

Another difference between these two forms of murder can be found in the different responses they provoke within the community. Typically, when a mass murder takes place, the immediate community, as well as the rest of the nation, is informed, and expressions of alarm at the slaughter of innocent victims quickly follow. The impact is immediate. The panic in the community is direct and severe, but short-lived. This is not the case with serial murder, which can disrupt community life for long periods. In Seattle, for example, residents have been terrorized for almost 10 years in the wake of the murders of more than 45 young women, some prostitutes, some not. In one large midwestern city, more than 40 unsolved homicides have instilled fear in the community. Unlike in cases of mass murder, there is no perceived end when serial murders occur.

The perpetrators of mass murder and of serial murder are also very different. The mass murderer is often perceived to be a demented, mentally ill person. People interviewed on television about a mass murderer after the fact often say that the killer had been seeing a mental health professional, had been on medication, had been threatening fellow employees, or the like. More research may show an early pattern that may be predictive of a mass murderer personality; thus far, however, this has not been researched adequately (Dietz, 1986; Hickey, 1991; Norris, 1988). It often seems that if only we had the expertise and the resources, we would be able to detect such people before they kill. This is not the case with the serial murderer. Ted Bundy, Gerald Stano, Randy Craft, and others like them were all persons who were not easily discernible as dangerous. They walked into the lives of many, often invited, and dispatched them with little concern. Such cases can cause great social paranoia, because individuals perceive themselves to be personally vulnerable. Episodes of mass murder do not seem to inspire this same sense of fear and anxiety.

INCIDENCE OF MASS MURDER

Mass murder is neither a strictly American nor a modern phenomenon; such cases are spread across history and have taken place all over the world. In recent times it seems that mass murder has increased, but it is unclear whether the incidence of mass murder has actually risen or whether we are now simply better able to detect and thus report it. Some specific modern cases of mass murder are described below; Table 5.1 presents a list of mass murders dating from 1949.

In July 1966, Richard Speck entered a Chicago apartment occupied by nine student nurses. Methodically, brutally, and coldly selecting one victim after another, Speck led eight of the young women one at a time into a room and then sexually assaulted and murdered them. Thinking that he had killed all of

TABLE 5.1

Modern Mass Murders or Suspected Mass Murderers

Year	State	Murderer (or Suspected Murderer)[a]	Death Toll
1949	New Jersey	Howard Unruh	shot 13 neighbors
1950	Texas	William Cook	shot 5 family members
1955	Colorado	John Graham	bomb on a plane, 44 died
1959	Kansas	Richard Hickock	stabbed/shot 4 members of Culter family
1959	Kansas	Perry Smith	stabbed/shot 4 members of Culter family
1966	Illinois	Richard Speck	stabbed/strangled 8 student nurses
1966	Texas	Charles Whitman	shot 16, mostly students
1966	Arizona	Robert Smith	shot 5 women in a beauty salon
1969	California	Charles Watson	stabbed 9 persons for Charles Manson
1969	California	Patricia Krenwinkel	stabbed 9 persons for Charles Manson
1969	California	Linda Kasabian	stabbed 7 persons for Charles Manson
1969	California	Susan Atkins	stabbed 9 persons for Charles Manson
1970	North Carolina	Jeffrey MacDonald	stabbed 3 family members
1971	New Jersey	John List	shot 5 family members
1973	Georgia	Carl Isaacs	shot 5 members of a family
1973	Georgia	Billy Isaacs	shot 5 members of a family
1974	Louisiana	Mark Essex	shot 9, mostly police officers
1974	New York	Ronald DeFeo	shot 6 family members
1975	Florida	Bill Ziegler	shot 4 adults in a store
1975	Ohio	James Ruppert	shot 11 family members
1976	California	Edward Allaway	shot 7 coworkers
1977	New York	Frederick Cowan	shot 6 coworkers
1978	Guyana	Jim Jones	poisoned/shot 912 cult members
1980	Georgia	Wayne Coleman	shot and beat 6 people
1982	Pennsylvania	George Banks	shot 13 family members and acquaintances
1983	Louisiana	Michael Perry	shot 5 family members
1983	Washington	Willie Mak	shot 13 people in the head
1983	Washington	Benjamin Ng	shot 13 people in the head
1984	California	James Huberty	shot 21 people at McDonald's
1985	Pennsylvania	Sylvia Seigrist	shot several people at a mall, 2 died

continued

TABLE 5.1
Continued

Year	State	Murderer (or Suspected Murderer)[a]	Death Toll
1986	Oklahoma	Patrick Sherrill	shot 14 coworkers
1986	Arkansas	Ronald Simmons	shot 16 family members
1987	Florida	William Cruse	shot 6 people at a mall
1988	Minnesota	David Brown	axed 4 family members
1988	California	Richard Farley	shot 7 people in a computer company
1988	California	Patrick Purdy	shot 5 children in a school playground
1988	North Carolina	Michael Hayes	shot 4 neighbors
1989	Kentucky	Joseph Wesbecker	shot 8 coworkers
1990	Michigan	Lawrence DeLisle	drowned his 4 children
1990	Florida	James Pugh	shot 13 in an auto loan company
1990	New York	Julio Gonzalez	set a fire in a night club, 87 died
1991	Michigan	Ilene Russell	set a fire, 4 adults and 1 child died
1991	Ohio	Kim Chandler	shot her 3 children
1991	Kentucky	Michael Brunner	shot girlfriend and her 2 children
1991	New Jersey	Joseph Harris	shot 4 people in a post office
1991	New York	Andrew Brooks	shot his father and 3 men
1991	Hawaii	Orlando Ganal	shot 4 people, including his in-laws
1991	Texas	George Hennard	shot 22 people in a restaurant
1991	Iowa	Gang Lu	shot 5 college officials and students
1991	New Hampshire	James Colbert	strangled wife, suffocated 3 daughters
1991	Kentucky	Robert Daigneau	shot wife and 3 strangers
1991	Michigan	Thomas McIlwane	shot 3 children
1991	Florida	Curtis Windom	shot girlfriend and 2 adults
1992	Alabama	Jason Williams	shot 3 family members, 1 other adult

a. In some cases, the person named here may not have been charged with all the victims shown in the death toll because of the expense of further trials or lack of direct evidence to assure conviction. In some cases, for example, a person may be charged with only one murder even though police and the courts believe he or she is responsible for more. Also, a few of the people listed here have not yet gone to trial.

the young women in the apartment, and losing count that there were truly nine, he calmly walked out the front door and disappeared. One surviving young woman, however, had hidden under a bed. After Speck left, she screamed hysterically until help arrived. He was captured almost immediately by the Chicago police. He was tried and convicted and received multiple life sentences. Escaping the death penalty, he recently died in an Illinois prison.

Charles Whitman, another mass murderer, confessed to his college counselor that he had an overwhelming urge to kill people. The counselor, not sensing the immediacy of Whitman's condition, scheduled an appointment for him the next day. After leaving the office, Whitman went to his mother's home and killed her. He then arrived at his own apartment and killed his young wife. The next day, Whitman climbed to the top of a tower on the campus of the University of Texas at Austin and for 96 minutes shot indiscriminately at passersby. He shot 46 persons; 16 died. Whitman was finally shot by a police officer. The medical examination searched for a biological explanation for his condition. Doctors examined his brain for a tumor, hoping to find one that would explain Whitman's violent behavior, but no conclusive medical evidence was found (Hickey, 1991, p. 4).

Joseph Wesbecker was on disability leave from his job with Standard Gravure, a printing company in Louisville, Kentucky, when he entered the company building in September 1990 looking for supervisors. A mental patient still in therapy and under medication for periods of depression, he had previously mentioned to several coworkers that someday he would kill his bosses (Scanlon & Wolfson, 1989, pp. 1, 13). Carrying a bag under one arm containing several assault weapons as well as ammunition, he got off an elevator and immediately fatally wounded three persons (one a female friend of the first author), and then shot four more fellow employees before he finally killed himself.

In the late 1980s, in Stockton, California, Patrick Purdy drove to the Cleveland Elementary School playground, got out of his car with a gun, set the car on fire, and then walked to the side of the playground and opened fire on children playing there. After killing five children, he killed himself (Caputo, 1989;

"Death on the Playground," 1989; "Slaughter in a School Yard," 1989).

Perhaps one of the most infamous cases of mass murder is that of James Oliver Huberty. A skilled worker for the Babcock and Wilcox Company in Massilon, Ohio, Huberty was laid off from his job as a welder because of deteriorating economic conditions in northeast Ohio at the time. Moving to California, Huberty and his wife and two daughters settled in a working-class neighborhood. Gaining employment as a security officer, a job for which he was "overqualified," he soon found himself again unemployed. According to an interview Mrs. Huberty later gave, the morning of July 18, 1984, started off quietly enough (Home Box Office, 1988). The family went to the San Diego Zoo and later stopped for lunch at a McDonald's restaurant a half block from the Huberty apartment. After a lunch of Chicken McNuggets, fries, and a Coke, Huberty left the restaurant with his family. Mrs. Huberty stated that she was tired from the morning excursion to the zoo and had plans to go to the local grocery store for food for dinner. She decided to take an afternoon nap. While she was lying down in the bedroom, her husband came in and told her he was "going to hunt humans." He often said things to get her upset, and this time she decided that whatever he said it was not going to bother her. He kissed her good-bye, armed himself with weapons he kept in the apartment, walked out the front door, and turned right. Walking into McDonald's, he started firing, shooting 40 persons and killing 21. Huberty was eventually killed by a police sharpshooter from a building across the street.

What kind of a man would walk into a fast-food restaurant and shoot innocent persons? An angry man. A disenfranchised man. A man who believed that the world had done him a great disservice. Huberty perhaps reflected back on his life and saw failure after failure. There was evidence of his rage in his past behavior. In his home in Ohio, Huberty practiced shooting his gun into the basement wall. He kept a cache of weapons, and on more than one occasion he pointed a rifle at his neighbors from his back yard. He never fired, but he nonetheless frightened his neighbors continually. Forced to leave a job in Ohio after 15 years of faithful service, losing several homes and apartment houses in Ohio, he migrated to California only to lose a job there. Huberty fought back at a society he believed had treated him unjustly. But why did he murder innocent people, strangers? Clearly they were not responsible for his problems. Maybe they represented something to him that he was not; happy, contented to be with friends and relatives, somewhere he wanted to be but could not. Such ideas often rest within the mind of the mass murderer (see Holmes & Holmes, 1992).

CLASSIFICATION OF MASS MURDERERS

As with many forms of human conduct, sociologists and other social and behavioral scientists have attempted to organize the behaviors of mass murderers into social constructs. Such constructs are often based upon behavioral dynamics, motivations, victim characteristics and the methodology used in victim selection, locus of motivations (or the force behind the motivations), and anticipated rewards (Holmes & De Burger, 1988, pp. 46-60). In the following subsections we discuss these elements as they apply to mass murderers.

Behavioral Background: Basic Sources

It is unclear what causes some people to become mass murderers. It may be true that mass murderers are as different from nonmurderers as are serial killers, but it is also undoubtedly true that the etiology of their behavior is different from that of serial killers.

There appear to be three "root causes" in the development of the mass murderer. As Levin and Fox (1985, pp. 35-39) point out, multicidal offenders' behavior cannot easily be explained by simple biological factors. Biological anomalies—whether brain disorders, problems caused by blows to the head (Norris, 1988), or chemical imbalances—do not explain a person's total personality and behavior (Podolsky, 1964). The same can be said of socioeconomic factors. The factors that were often described as "root causes" of delinquency in the late 1960s—poverty, female-headed families, and so on—do not explain or account for all delinquency, and no list of any such factors can explain mass murder. The following statement about serial murderers is applicable to mass murderers as well:

> "Bad" neighborhoods, economic stress, family instability, and violence in the culture do not directly produce serial murderers. Out of a cohort that experiences the worst possible combinations of social stresses, relatively few will engage in outright criminal behavior and fewer still will become homicidal. (Holmes & De Burger, 1988, p. 48)

The elements that combine to create a mass murderer are as complex as those that result in a serial or spree murderer. Personality and behavior come about from a unique combination of biology, sociology, and personal psychology.

Dr. Donald Lunde (1976), a well-respected psychiatrist, boldly states that the majority of mass murderers suffer from psychosis and should be considered insane. He suggests that two kinds of personalities account for the overwhelming majority of mass murderers: (a) the paranoid schizophrenic, someone who displays an aggressive and suspicious demeanor and experiences hallucinations and/or delusions, and (b) the sexual sadist, whose murders are characterized by killing, torturing, and/or mutilating the victims in order to achieve sexual gratification. Lunde's second category does not fit the definition of mass murderer we are concerned with here; rather, it describes what we refer to as a "hedonistic" serial killer (Holmes & De Burger, 1985, 1988). It is likely that Lunde's categories were not intended to describe only the type of mass murderer under discussion here; he appears to have been concerned with multicide in general.

One further difference between mass murderers and serial murders should be noted. According to our own analysis of more than 40 cases of mass murder, usually, unless the mass murderer is a mercenary or has committed murder for revenge, he or she is willing to die at the scene of the crime, either committing suicide or forcing those in authority to kill him or her. (In cases involving disciple killers, their fates lie in the wishes of their leaders.) In contrast, there is overwhelming evidence that serial murderers do not wish to be apprehended; they wish to continue their killing, for whatever motivation impels them to do so.

Victim Characteristics

Victim traits do not appear to be a crucial element in mass murder. Victims are simply in the wrong place at the wrong time. The customers at that McDonald's restaurant had no role in Huberty's targeting them for mass murder other than simply being there.

Motivation

Another element used in the categorization of an individual mass murderer is motivation. What is the motivation for a person to commit such an atrocity as the murder of a large number of persons? This is not an easy question to address adequately. A partial answer rests in the location of the motivation, that is, whether it is intrinsic or extrinsic. For example, is the person motivated by something deep within, something over which the person has no control? This is a common statement heard in our interviews with multicidal offenders, such as serial killers. These killers identify an entity within their personalities that impels them to kill. It is indeed a small part, but this 1% can take over the 99% (Michaud & Aynesworth, 1983). This does not appear to be true with mass murderers.

Sometimes the motivating force rests outside the individual, something that commands the killing. Charlie Manson's control over Tex Watson and the other members of "the Family" to kill Sharon Tate, Steven Parent, Abigail Folger, Voytek Frykowski, and Jay Sebring, and the second night to go to the home of Leno and Rosemary LaBianca, is an example of an external locus of motivation. The instruction of Manson to kill rested outside the personalities of the killers themselves.

With James Huberty the motivation to kill rested within Huberty himself. For myriad reasons, ranging perhaps from occupational and social class frustrations to many other stresses, Huberty killed, not because someone commanded that he do so. Rather, he apparently believed that society was operating against him; he perceived himself to be a victim of social injustice. However, we will never know exactly how or why he chose to vent his rage on the strangers who happened to be at McDonald's that day.

Anticipated Gain

The murderer's anticipated gains must also be considered. What is the person hoping to realize by carrying out the act of murder? Does he or she want to get revenge on former supervisors at the workplace because of a poor job performance rating? Or is a monetary reward anticipated, as when an arson-for-profit scheme results in the deaths of innocent persons? Although murderers' anticipated gains can vary a great deal, the result is the same: Innocent people die.

Anticipated gains may be thought of as either expressive (psychological) or instrumental (material). Examination of the killer's perceived gains is important in the consideration of the type of mass killer, not only from a law enforcement point of view but also from a social/behavioral perspective.

Spatial Mobility

Geographic or spatial mobility plays a strong role in the categorization of the four types of serial killers: visionary, mission, hedonistic, and power/control (Holmes & De Burger, 1985; see Chapter 6). However, like victim selection, this element does not play a critical role in mass murder. Unless involved in mass murder for pay (e.g., arsonists or mercenaries), most mass murderers are geographically stable. The various cases of mass killers described above clearly illustrate this point.

An apparent exception to this usual trait of geographic stability is the case of the disciple killer. This type of killer, who has fallen under the spell of a charismatic leader, is often a runaway or a castoff from society. Such a murderer may not be indigenous to the area where he or she kills. However, the domicile of the disciple killer is often semipermanent, and victims tend to be people who live in the same locale as the killers and the leader.

TYPOLOGY OF MASS MURDERERS

The development of a typology of mass murderers is an arduous task. The first decision concerns the base number of killings necessary to consider a case one of mass murder; as noted above, we have already settled on the number three. The further requirement that the killings occurred at one time and in one place is easily met; there are many such cases.

The next task at hand is the development of a taxonomy predicated upon the elements of basic sources, victim characteristics, motivation, anticipated gain, and spatial mobility. There are also other elements to consider, such as type of weapon used, life-style of the killer, relational closeness or affinity of the victims, and personal mental/physical health of the killer.

The Disciple

The disciple killer follows the dictates of a charismatic leader. The Manson Family provides many excellent examples of this type of mass killer. Consider Leslie Van Houten: A former high school cheerleader and beauty queen, this young woman of 16 fell under the spell of Charles Manson, as did many others, including Lynette Fromme, Tex Watson, and Bobby Beausoleil (Livesey, 1980).

What caused these "nice, normal" young people of the peace generation to become ruthless and merciless killers? There is no easy answer. We do know that disciple killers' victim selection is left to the discretion of the leader. Manson allegedly told his followers to kill those who happened to be at the former rented home at 10050 Cielo Drive. This was the former residence of Doris Day's son, Terry Melcher, and actress Candice Bergen (Bugliosi, 1975, p. 4). The disciple killer's motivation for mass murder rests outside the killer.

The anticipated gain of the disciple killer is psychological or expressive: The leader of the group demands the action, and the killer wants the acceptance of the leader. This psychological acceptance is paramount in the need hierarchy of the disciple killer. Money, revenge, and sex are neither motivating factors nor anticipated gains. The disciple killer desires psychological approbation and feels he or she deserves it for carrying out the wishes of the leader. This same scenario was repeated by the followers of Jim Jones in the massacre at Jonestown in Guyana. The hoped-for gain of the disciple killer is generally expressive (psychological) rather than instrumental (material).

Manson Family Members and Acquaintances

Charles Manson	Jesus Christ, Satan, the Devil, the leader of the Family
Susan Atkins	involved in the Tate and LaBianca killings as well as other cases; also known as Sadie Mae Glutz, Sexy Sadie, Sharon King, Donna Kay Powell
Bobby Beausoleil	involved in the Gary Hinman killing; also known as Cupid, Jasper, Cherub, Robert Lee Hardy, Jason Lee Daniels
Mary Brunner	first girl to join the Family; may have been involved in the Hinman killing; also known as Marioche, Och, Mother Mary, Mary Manson, Linda Dee Moser
James Craig	pleaded guilty to being an accessory after the fact in two murders; formerly a state prison escapee
Lynette Fromme	one of Manson's earliest followers; assumed leadership after Manson was arrested; also known as Squeaky, Elizabeth Elaine Williamson; currently in prison for attempting to assassinate the president of the United States
Catherine Gillies	granddaughter of the owner of the Myers Ranch, where the Family lived for a time; wanted to accompany Watson and others the night the LaBiancas were killed; also known as Capistrano, Cappy, Catherine Myers, Patti Sue, Patricia Anne Burke
Sandra Good	a Family member; also known as Sandy
Steven Grogan	was with the murderers the night of the LaBianca killings; also involved in the Hinman killing and possibly involved in the attempted murder of a prosecution witness in the trial against Manson; also known as Clem Tufts
Gary Hinman	befriended the Family and was murdered by them
Linda Kasabian	accompanied the killers on the nights of the Tate and LaBianca murders; was a witness for the prosecution
Patricia Krenwinkel	involved in the Tate and LaBianca killings; also known as Katie, Marnie Reeves, Big Patty
Leslie Van Houten	involved in the LaBianca killings; also known as LuLu, Leslie Marie Sankston, Louella Alexandria, Leslie Owens
Charles Watson	involved in the Tate and LaBianca killings; also known as Tex or Texas Charlie

SOURCE: Some information shown here is from Bugliosi (1975).

Spatial mobility is also an element in the disciple killer's profile. Typically, the killer's acts of violence are carried out near the location of the leader. So a disciple killer is rarely a traveler in the same sense as is a geographically transient serial killer. However, as noted above, the disciple killer follows the leader, and is unlikely to be originally from the general area in which the crimes are committed.

The types of weapons used in mass murder by disciple killers usually are restricted to hand weapons—knives, guns, and the like. In the Jonestown case, the weapon was poison.

Disciple killers, unlike other mass murderers, do not appear to have a general dislike of the world around them, nor do they believe themselves to be in a situation from which they can remove themselves only by killing. Disciple killers murder because of the effect their leaders have on them. Their victims, typically strangers, are selected by their leaders, so victim selection is not a factor for disciple killers. In a way, disciple killers may be compared with soldiers who kill prisoners of war, not out of fear for their own lives, but because of their dedication to the message of the leader. Such killers may feel themselves to be relieved of a certain amount of personal responsibility by this scenario.

The Family Annihilator

Dietz (1986) describes the family annihilator type of mass murderer in an article titled "Mass, Serial and Sensational Homicides." This murderer kills an entire family at one time, and may even kill the family pet. According to Dietz, the family annihilator is the senior male in the family, often has a history of alcohol abuse, and exhibits great periods of depression.

The motivation for this murderer lies within the psyche of the person. Often feeling alone, anomic, and helpless, this killer launches a campaign of violence typically against those who share his home. Because of the despair in his own life, the killer wishes to change the situation, and reacts in this most bizarre fashion.

Geographic mobility plays a very small role in this type of mass murder. The family annihilator tends to live in the area in which he commits his crimes. Usually a lifelong member of the community, he chooses to end the life of his family for reasons that

TABLE 5.2

Traits of Different Types of Mass Murderers

	Disciple	Family Annihilator	Pseudo-commando	Disgruntled Employee	Set-and-Run
Motivation					
intrinsic		X	X	X	
extrinsic	X				X
Anticipated gain					
expressive	X	X	X	X	
instrumental					X
Victim selection					
random	X		X		X
nonrandom		X		X	
Victim relationship					
affiliative		X		X	
strangers	X		X		X
Spatial mobility					
stable		X	X	X	
transient	X				X
Victim traits					
specific					
nonspecific	X	X	X	X	X

are unclear not only to investigators but to the killer as well. In Minnesota in 1988, David Brown allegedly axed 4 family members to death; there was no clear reason for his actions. In 1982, George Banks was arrested for shooting 13 family members and relatives for unknown reasons; the family was well known in the community. Ronald Simmons, recently executed in Arkansas for his crimes, killed 16 members of his family in 1986.

The Pseudocommando

Dietz (1986) also describes the pseudocommando, a mass murderer preoccupied with weaponry. Often this kind of killer, usually male, stockpiles exotic weapons in his home. Assault weapons, machine guns, even hand grenades are not unknown to this mass murderer. The pseudocommando's mass homicide occurs usually after a long period of deliberation and careful planning.

There is no clear understanding as to the exact etiology of the pseudocommando personality. Certainly there are social components to this behavior; the killer's world plays an integral part in his behavior. But the pseudocommando lashes out at society in a most grotesque way. Something in his world is not correct and he decides to "teach the world a lesson."

For the pseudocommando, as for most mass murderers, victim characteristics do not appear to be important in the victim selection process. Unlike the serial killer, who may have a shoe fetish or who may select victims with particular hairstyles, the victims of the pseudocommando may simply be in the wrong place at the wrong time. When Huberty walked into McDonald's in 1984, the only relationship he had with the victims was that they were all in the same place at the same time.

The motivation of the pseudocommando appears to rest within the psyche of the killer. Something inside the person impels him to carry out his massacre. There is nothing outside the personality that demands that he kill.

The anticipated gain of the pseudocommando is twofold. First, the activity of the mass kill calls attention to whatever issue the killer believes to be important. In the case of Huberty, the economic condition of the nation that resulted in his moving to California from Ohio was certainly one of the reasons that he committed the act. The second hoped-for gain is less understandable: The killer wants his name to live in infamy. Most of us recognize the name of James Huberty; how many know any of the names of the 40 victims? Most of us recall the name of Charles Whitman; can you name any of his victims?

Geographic mobility does not appear to be a significant element among pseudocommandos. Huberty had moved to California, Whitman lived in Texas—both killed near where they were living at the time. The pseudocommando does not seem to go far from home to commit mass murder.

The Disgruntled Employee

Disgruntled employees who kill have often been dismissed from their jobs or placed on some form of medical leave or disability. These mass killers are frequently receiving psychiatric counseling, and many see themselves to be suffering great personal injustices that are beyond their control. They retaliate for the wrongs they perceive by going to their former places of employment, searching out those they believe have wronged them, and killing those persons (and often others as well). This scenario fits the case of Joseph Wesbecker exactly, and also that of Patrick Sherrill. In 1986, Sherrill returned to the post office where he was an employee. Looking for supervisors, he started firing into the rooms and corridors of the post office, wounding and killing indiscriminately. Even though his primary motive was to kill supervisors, he actually wounded and killed many coworkers ("Crazy Pat's Revenge," 1986; "10 Minutes of Madness," 1986).

The psychological sources of the disgruntled employee's mentality are unknown. Very often these persons are on some form of medication and/or are receiving counseling or psychotherapy, and they are often diagnosed as paranoid.

The victim selection process of the disgruntled employee who kills is initially nonrandom. This mass murderer seeks a particular group of persons to kill, usually supervisors in the killer's former workplace. However, once inside the workplace, the killer often will randomly fire into rooms, shooting anyone who happens to be there.

Disgruntled employees' motivation to kill rests within their desire to "right a wrong." They kill to call attention to wrongs that they perceive to have been directed at and carried out against them. There is no external locus of motivation, as there is for the disciple killer.

The anticipated gains for disgruntled employees who kill are psychological. There is no money to be realized, no social justice issues to be exposed, nothing outside the world of work and the injustices that were committed there.

The spatial mobility of this kind of killer is usually very limited. Often, the person has been employed for years with the same company and has lived in the same community for that same period or longer. Wesbecker, for example, worked for the Standard Gravure Company for more than 15 years. Sherrill was a postal worker for more than a decade. Wesbecker was a native of Louisville, Kentucky; Sherrill had lived in the same community for more than 20 years.

The danger the disgruntled employee poses for citizens in the community at large is obviously quite limited; of course, this is of no comfort to the families of this killer's victims.

The Set-and-Run Killer

Another type of mass murderer described by Dietz (1986) is the set-and-run killer. Operating sometimes out of a motive for revenge, sometimes seeking anonymous infamy, and sometimes killing simply for profit, this type of murderer is qualitatively different from those discussed above.

As noted earlier, most mass killers either commit suicide at the scenes of their crimes or force those in law enforcement to kill them. This is not true with set-and-run killers. These murderers employ techniques that will allow them to escape before the deaths they cause actually occur. For example, a set-and-run killer may plant a bomb in a building, setting a timing device so the murderer can be far removed from the scene when the explosion occurs. The person who poisons food products or medicines, placing the containers back on store shelves to be sold later, is also a set-and-run killer. This murderer does not directly observe the consequences of his or her acts; he or she may be across town or even in another country when the results become a part of the community's awareness.

Depending on the individual set-and-run killer's motivation, victim selection will vary. For example, if a person sets a building on fire so that he or the building owner who hired him can collect insurance money, and there are people inside the building who die as a result, the characteristics of these victims were of no significance in the crime; the anticipated gain of the arsonist is monetary. There is no psychological motivation in such a case, no attempt to "show the world" anything. This kind of motivation lies not within the personality of the killer but in instrumental gain.

In some instances, the victim of the set-and-run killer may be once removed. Take, for example, a person who tampers with a food product made by Company X. Five people may purchase and eat the food, and all five may die, but in the mind of the killer, Company X is the victim, because the company will be

seen to be at fault for the deaths. The motivation here is psychological; the killer is getting revenge on Company X for some
perceived wrong. The anticipated gain is also psychological; no
money is realized. A further psychological payoff for the killer
may be the fact that Company X may even lose money, because
some customers will no longer purchase its products, fearing
they are unsafe.

Because set-and-run killers are not present when their killings
actually occur, they are very difficult to apprehend. Knowledge
about the motivations, anticipated gains, and victim characteristics (when the victims are once removed) of these killers is
crucial to those who hope to understand and possibly apprehend them.

CONCLUSION

The incidence of mass murder, in the United States and abroad,
does not appear to be decreasing. During our writing of this
chapter, two cases of mass murder have occurred, one in the
United States and the other in Australia. There will always certainly
be persons who will be motivated by personal, economic, or social
pressures and who will arm themselves with a variety of weapons
to carry out their acts. This is not an easy situation to accept, in no
small part because of the perceived vulnerability it creates. We
cannot protect ourselves from deranged mass murderers, or even,
for that matter, from very rational mercenary set-and-run killers.
This is unsettling, to understate the point. The mass murderer may
strike at any time and in any place.

What can we do? Some say that effective gun control legislation may be an answer. Certainly, if rigorously and scrupulously
enforced, such laws may deter some mass killers who would
resort to their own previously purchased weaponry to carry out
their crimes. It would also deter those who recognize their
feelings, plan their crimes, and then purchase weapons. Unfortunately, however, this scenario is not very common. It is unlikely that gun control can be society's answer to the problem
of mass murder.

Aside from paid killers, as discussed, the majority of mass
murderers display danger signs before they undertake their

crimes. If we can become more aware of these signs, if those in the mental health profession, for example, know the red flags that may signal the danger, then some of these acts can be circumvented before innocent lives are lost. This appears to be the best plan for the reduction of the horrendous crime of mass murder. Can it ever be completely eradicated? We can only hope.

6

Serial Murder

Serial murder may be the crime of the 1990s (Holmes, 1991; Holmes, De Burger, & Holmes, 1990). Stories of serial killings have long been rampant in the media, especially since the middle 1970s, and serial murder has become a part of North America's consciousness. Volumes of information have appeared on this topic, on a serious academic level (e.g., Gollmar, 1982; Hickey, 1991; Holmes, 1990, 1991; Holmes & De Burger, 1985, 1988; Norris, 1988; Ressler, Burgess, & Douglas, 1988; Schechter, 1990) as well as on a more popular level, in narrative format. Most of these popular reports lack serious documentation and rely almost solely upon police reports, imagined narrations, and others' research efforts. Both types of published accounts of serial murder typically concentrate only on men, because the overwhelming number of serial killers are men. For example, in one study of 47 serial killers, only 3 were females (Holmes & De Burger, 1988). Of these, 2 had killed family members and the other murdered as a team with her male lover. In other studies, no women serial killers are mentioned (e.g., Levin & Fox, 1985; Ressler et al., 1988).

A serial killer is defined as someone who murders at least three persons in more than a 30-day period. These killings typically involve one victim per episode. Mass murder, in contrast, involves the killing of a number of persons in one place at one time. Examples of mass murderers include James Oliver Huberty and Richard Speck. Huberty shot 40 people in a McDonald's restaurant in San Diego, and 21 died. Richard Speck killed 8 student nurses in one night in Chicago in the mid-1960s.

Serial murderers such as Ted Bundy, Angelo Buono, Douglas Clark, Wayne Williams, David Berkowitz, Kenneth Bianchi, Randy Craft, and Donald Harvey strike fear in the minds of many Americans. Martha Beck, Dorothea Puente, Belle Gunness, and Genene Jones are but a few of the females who have been suspected to be serial murderers. As noted above, women are seldom considered in discussions of serial offenders, although in recent years there has been a great increase in the number of women who kill serially. These women add a dramatic and disconcerting dimension to the social problem of serial murder. One reason for this may be that women traditionally have been viewed as basically incapable of the kinds of acts that have been attributed to serial killers.

Serial murder is difficult for the average person to comprehend, perhaps in part because of the individual risk it represents. It is hard to think of oneself as at risk of becoming a victim of such a brutal type of offender. Further, the damage done by the serial killer extends beyond the immediate victim to the victim's family members and friends, who suffer horribly as a result of such a crime.

More "traditional" forms of homicide typically involve a personal or tangential relationship between the victim and the offender, such as when a woman kills her abusive husband, or an argument outside a bar turns violent. In serial murder, as in mass murder, becoming a victim may very well depend on nothing more than being in the wrong place at the wrong time; anyone can be a victim. There is no personal confrontation in serial murder; there is no personal relationship, as exists in other forms of homicide. This makes serial murder all the more difficult to understand. The knowledge that we are all equally vulnerable leads not only to a shared sensation of controlled panic, but to a growing fascination with serial murder.

SERIAL MURDER
OUTSIDE THE UNITED STATES

Many people mistakenly believe that serial murder is a strictly American phenomenon (Jenkins, 1988). On the contrary, serial murder is not confined to this continent. For instance, there have been many murderers in the history of Europe that fit the operational definition of serial killer. One of the most famous, of course, was Jack the Ripper.

In the summer of 1888, Londoners were alarmed by a series of murders of prostitutes. The news accounts of the time contained gory details of the murders. Even though "respectable" women perhaps believed they were not in danger, both men and women were startled and outraged by the acts of the killer who came to be known as "Jack the Ripper."

The first murder took place on the night of August 7, 1888. The victim, Martha Turner, died as the result of more than 39 knife wounds. The cuts made were so expertly done that an attending physician who also performed the autopsy said that the killer had to have some knowledge of anatomy. Mary Ann Nicholls became the second victim 24 days later. Five of her front teeth had been removed in a manner that suggested the killer was left-handed. One week later, Annie Chapman became the third victim. The police found coins and brass rings at her feet, apparently laid there by her killer. The fourth victim, Elizabeth Stride, died when her windpipe was cut out; when police found her, she was still bleeding. The fifth victim was Catherine Eddowes. Her body was found on the same night as Stride's. Her ears had been surgically removed. The sixth, and some believe the last, victim was Mary Kelly, who was pregnant when she died. She had been disemboweled, and pieces of her flesh were placed on nails on the wall next to her body. In her apartment's fireplace, police found evidence of a woman's hat, other clothing, and a piece of velvet. Her body was found on November 9, 1888.

The case of Jack the Ripper has never been resolved, and it still attracts the attention of those interested in serial murder. The police in England have maintained an ongoing interest in Jack the Ripper's true identity. A list of suspects has been developed, none of whom was ever arrested. The list includes the Duke of Clarence, a surgeon who contracted a venereal disease from a prostitute; James Stephens, a friend of the Duke of Clarence and son of a judge in London; and Severin Klosowski, who had been a doctor's assistant in the Russian army. Many believe that the strongest case can be made against Montague

TABLE 6.1
Serial Murderers Outside the United States

Years	Name	Country	Number of Victims
1430	Giles De Raise	France	800+
1600	Sawney Bean	Scotland	1,500+
1790-1840	Thuggee Burham	India	931
1800	Andreas Bichel	Bavaria	50+
1820	William Burke	Scotland	32
1890	Alfred Deeming	Austria, England	20
1894-1897	Joseph Vacher	France	10-20
1898-1901	Ludwig Tessor	Germany	30+
1918-1922	Fritz Haarman	England	30-40
1924	Carl Deenke	Poland	30+
1941-1946	Marcel Petiot	France	63
1943	Bruno Ludke	Germany	85
1945-1963	Teofilo Rojas	Colombia	592+
1953-1963	Efrain Gonzales	Colombia	117
1962	Lucian Staniak	Poland	20
1969-1984	Daniel Barbosa	Brazil	71
1977	Pedro Lopez	Ecuador	300+
1977-1980	Arn Finn Nesset	Norway	22-25
1987	"Locksmith"	Russia	33

SOURCE: Data compiled from material in Hickey (1991).

John Druitt. This young man, an athlete and a graduate of Oxford, an educated attorney who failed to practice law before the courts in England, committed suicide within weeks of the last killing.

There has also been some speculation that the killer may have been a woman, a midwife, who perhaps had some vindictive feelings toward prostitutes. This theory has no basis in investigations done by the police, especially given that witnesses stated that some of the victims had last been seen with a man who was about five feet, six inches tall, who wore a hat, a long coat, and spats (Noguchi, 1985; Wilson & Oden, 1987).

There have been other serial killers in Europe as well as in other parts of the world. Table 6.1 lists the names of some serial killers who have operated outside of the United States. The table includes only male killers thought to be responsible for 20 or more deaths; there have been many other serial killers who killed fewer than 20, and women have not been absent from the roll of serial murderers, either outside or within the United States (female serial killers in general will be covered in more depth later in this chapter). Clearly, serial murder can be found all over the world.

SERIAL KILLERS IN THE UNITED STATES

The list of serial killers in the United States reads like an unholy litany. Albert Fish, Ed Gein, Ted Bundy, Randy Craft, David Berkowitz, John Gacy, and Jeffrey Dahmer are but a few of the notorious serial killers who have made headlines in the North American news media. Table 6.2 lists many of the known serial killers who have been active in the United States since 1900. Descriptions of the crimes of a few of these killers are offered in this section.

Albert Fish was a notable mysoped (a sadistic pedophile) in New York state in the early part of the twentieth century. Thought to be responsible for the murder, mutilation, and cannibalism of scores of children, Fish was finally apprehended by the New York City Police Department for the kidnapping and murder of 10-year-old Grace Budd. When the police arrested Fish, he was cooking the bodily remains of the young girl on his kitchen stove (Schechter, 1990).

Fish had a previous criminal record. He had been arrested several years earlier for writing obscene letters to women whose names he had secured from personal ads. He had also been arrested previously for burglary. Preoccupied with thoughts of anthropophagy (cannibalism), coprolagnia (eating excrement), and urolagnia (drinking urine), this killer had been evaluated by a court-appointed psychiatrist and found to be legally sane. He was subsequently released from custody. After he was released from jail, he continued with his sexual aberrations. He urged several sexual partners to spank him as well as to urinate upon him and defecate into his mouth (Schechter, 1990).

After Fish was found guilty in the murder of Grace Budd, he was sentenced to die in the electric chair at Sing Sing. After his execution, for which he helped the guards strap him into the electric chair, an autopsy revealed that he had 29 sewing needles

text continued on page 102

TABLE 6.2
Alleged Serial Murderers in the United States

Years	Name	Location	Victim Characteristics
1900-1939	Joseph Briggen	California	hired hands
	Alonzo Robinson	various states	men, women
	Billy Gohl	Washington	sailors
	Belle Gunness	Indiana	suitors, husbands
	Louise Peete	California	men, women
	Mary Eleanor Smith	Washington	men
	Earl Smith	Washington	men
	Tillie Klimek	Illinois	husbands, suitors
	James Watson	Northwest	suitors
	Harry Powers	West Virginia	suitors, children
	Joseph Mumfre	Louisiana	Italian grocers
	Gordon Northcott	California	children
	Sarah Northcott	California	children
	Clarence Robinson	California	children
	Jane Toppan	Massachusetts	hospital patients
	Amy Archer-Gilligan	Connecticut	men, women
	Anna Hahn	Ohio	elderly male hospital patients
	Kate ("Ma") Barker	Midwest	adults
	Lloyd Barker	Midwest	adults
	Arthur Barker	Midwest	adults
	Fred Barker	Midwest	adults
	Herman Barker	Midwest	adults
	Bonnie Parker	Southwest	adults
	Clyde Barrow	Southwest	adults
	Johann Hoch	Illinois	wives
	Mary Creighton	New York	family, friends
	John Creighton	New York	family, friends
	Martha Wise	Ohio	family
1940-1959	Earle Nelson	several states	landladies
	Joseph Ball	Texas	wives, waitresses
	Carl Panzram	Connecticut	varied
	H. H. Mudgett	Illinois	varied
	Albert Fish	New York	children
	Jake Bird	Washington	females
	Mack Edwards	California	children
	Nannie Doss	Oklahoma	husbands, family
	Harvey Glatman	California	women
	Anjette Lyles	Georgia	husbands, women
	Kenneth Dudley	Florida	family (children)
	Irene Dudley	Florida	family (children)

continued

TABLE 6.2
Continued

Years	Name	Location	Victim Characteristics
	Douglas Gretzler	New York	young white boys
	William Steelman	New York	young white boys
	Melvin Rees	Maryland	young women
	Bill Heirens	Illinois	women
	Richard Biegenwald	New York, New Jersey	women
	Martha Beck	New York, Michigan	women
	Ray Fernandez	New York, Michigan	women
	Edward Gein	Wisconsin	women, children
1960s	Albert DeSalvo	Massachusetts	women
	Richard Tingle	Ohio	men, women
	Jerry Brudos	Oregon	young women
	Richard Marquette	Oregon	women
	Charles Schmid	Arizona	young girls
	Posteal Laskey	Ohio	women
	John Collins	Michigan	college women
	Janice Gibbs	Georgia	family
	Zodiac	California	men, women
1970s	Edmund Kemper	California	college women, mother
	Erno Soto	New York	young black males
	Harvey Carignan	Oregon, Washington	young women
	Salvatore Gravano	New York	varied (mob hits)
	Audrey Hilley	Alabama	husband, women, police officer
	Juan Corona	California	farm workers
	David Berkowitz	New York	women
	David Bullock	New York	men, women
	BTK Strangler	Kansas	men, women
	Richard Cottingham	New York	prostitutes
	Ted Bundy	10 states	women
	Herbert Mullin	California	varied
	John Wayne Gacy	Illinois	young men
	Gerald Eugene Stano	Florida	women
	Angelo Buono	California	women
	Kenneth Bianchi	California, Washington	women
	Dean Corll	Texas	men
	Wayne Henley	Texas	men
	Wayne Kearney	California	men
	Henry Lucas	several states	men, women
	Ottis Toole	several states	men, women
	William Bonin	California	men
	Carlton Gary	Georgia	elderly women

continued

TABLE 6.2
Continued

Years	Name	Location	Victim Characteristics
	Paul Knowles	7 states	men, women
	Joseph Fisher	several states	men, women
	Joseph Kallinger	Pennsylvania	son, young boy, a woman
	Gary and Thaddeus Lewington	Ohio	men, women
	Manuel Moore	California	white adults
	Larry Green	California	white adults
	Jessie Cooks	California	white adults
	J. C. Simon	California	white adults
	Velma Barfield	South Carolina	husband, mother, women
	Robert Reidan	New Jersey	women
	Richard Chad	California	men, women
	"The Babysitter"	Michigan	young children
	Paul Bateson	New York	homosexuals
1980s	Douglas Clark	California	prostitutes
	David Christopher	several states	black males
	Donald Gaskins	South Carolina	men, women
	Betty Lou Beets	Texas	husbands, one other man
	Mary Beth Tinning	New York	her children
	David Carpenter	Texas	women, a child, young men
	Coral Watts	several states	women
	Lawrence Bittaker	California	young women
	Ray Norris	California	young women
	Richard Chase	California	women, children
	Richard Angelo	California	hospital patients
	Gerald Gallego	California, Nevada	men, women
	Christine Gallego	California, Nevada	men, women
	Randy Woodfield	California, Washington, Oregon	women
	Robert Long	Florida	women
	Robert Hansen	Alaska	prostitutes
	Gary Bishop	Utah	young boys
	Wayne Williams	Georgia	young boys, girls, men
	Larry Eyler	Midwest	young men
	Richard Ramirez	California	varied
	Christopher Wilder	several states	young women
	Joseph Franklin	several states	young black males

continued

TABLE 6.2
Continued

Years	Name	Location	Victim Characteristics
	Terri Rachels	Georgia	hospital patients
	Genene Jones	Texas	hospital patients
	Christine Falling	Florida	children, one elderly man
	Sherman McCrary	several states	prostitutes
	Carl Taylor	several states	prostitutes
	Green River Killer	Washington	women
	San Diego Killer	California	women
	Beoria Simmons	Kentucky	women
	Donald Harvey	Kentucky, Ohio	hospital patients
	Calvin Jackson	New York	hotel guests
	Gary Heidnik	Pennsylvania	women
	Alton Coleman	several states	women
	Debra Brown	several states	women
	Robin Gecht	Illinois	women
	Edward Sprietzer	Illinois	women
	Andrew Kokaraleis	Illinois	women
	Thomas Kokaraleis	Illinois	women
	Leonard Lake	California	men and women hikers
	Charles Ng	California	men and women hikers
	Randy Craft	California	men
	Arthur Shawcross	New York	prostitutes
	Bobbie Sue Terrell	Florida	nursing home patients
	Dorothea Puente	California	boarders
	Anthony Joyner	Pennsylvania	nursing home patients
	Jeffrey Feltner	Florida	hospital patients
	Richard Diaz	California	hospital patients
	Robert Bedella	Missouri	young males
	Jane Bolding	Maryland	hospital patients
	Priscilla Ford	Nevada	men, women
	Troost Avenue Killer	Missouri	women, prostitutes
	Tied Up Murderer	Missouri	women, prostitutes
	Avenue Mutilator	Missouri	women, prostitutes
	Downtown Killer	Missouri	women, prostitutes
	Main Street Killer	Missouri	prostitutes
	John Joubert	Nebraska	young boys
	Nathaniel Code	Louisiana	men, women
	Richard Kuklinski	New York, New Jersey	varied (mob hits)

continued

TABLE 6.2
Continued

Years	Name	Location	Victim Characteristics
	Wayne Nance	several states	men, women
	Carroll Cole	Nevada, Texas	men, women
	Judias Buenoano	Florida	husband, boyfriend, son
	Donald Harding	several states	businessmen
	Richard Angelo	New York	men, women
1990s	Richard Berdella	Missouri	street people
	Brian Rosenfield	Florida	nursing home patients
	George Putt	Georgia	men, women
	Sean Sellers	Oklahoma	grocer, mother, stepfather
	Gilham Park Strangler	Missouri	women, prostitutes
	Miami (Ohio) Killer	Ohio	women
	Gainesville Killer	Florida	women, one man
	Westley Dodd	Oregon, Washington	young boys
	Ray and Faye Copeland	Missouri	farmhands
	Jeffrey Dahmer	Wisconsin	men, women
	Oscar Bolin	various states	women
	Leslie Warren	various states	women
	Aileen Wuornos	Florida	men
	Thrill Killer	California	store clerks
	Joseph Akin	Georgia	hospital patients
	Robert Foley	Kentucky, Ohio	men, women
	Michael St. Clair	various states	men, women
	Dennis Reese	various states	men, women
	Scott Cox	Oregon	women
	Kevin Garr	Virginia	women
	William Green	Texas	men, women
	Michael Lefthand	North Dakota, Wisconsin	men
	Manny Pardo	Florida	drug dealers
	Cathy Wood	Michigan	nursing home patients
	Gwen Graham	Michigan	nursing home patients
	Newark Killer	New Jersey	black females
	Leslie Allen Williams	Michigan	females

inserted into his penis and scrotum. This sex act of infibulation was obviously quite gratifying to him (Schechter, 1990).

Ed Gein was another bizarre serial murderer. In Plainfield, Wisconsin, Gein was known as a loner, strange and aloof to the townspeople. On the opening of deer-hunting season, Gein went into town for kerosene and a rifle. Entering the town's hardware store, he murdered the owner, Bernice Worden. The authorities quickly discovered her body hanging from a rafter in Gein's woodshed, dressed out as a slaughtered deer. They also found skulls placed on his bedposts, other skulls used as drinking cups, fingers in bowls, and a tanned, skinned face that he had used as a mask while baying at the full moon from his yard. An admitted cannibal, grave robber, and serial killer, Gein died of natural causes in a state mental hospital in 1984 (Gollmar, 1982).

Not all cases of serial murder involve such bizarre acts as those of Gein and Fish; others are more mundane. In any case, the acts of serialists, whether the unspeakable acts of Fish, Gein, John Gacy, Henry Lucas, and others, or the less bizarre murders of other killers, are perpetrated against victims who share no connection with their killers other than being unwittingly in the killers' "comfort zones," places where the killers feel at ease to do what they wish without interference.

INCIDENCE OF SERIAL MURDER

The stories of many infamous serial killers have been told through the mass media, both electronic and print. Chris Wilder was profiled in the television movie *Easy Prey*. Ted Bundy's story was related in a TV miniseries titled *The Deliberate Stranger*. Ken Bianchi's story was a two-hour program, *The Hillside Strangler.* Paperback books appear on newsstands almost weekly, telling the grisly stories: *Deranged* (about Albert Fish; Schechter, 1990), *The I-5 Killer* (about Randy Woodfield; Rule, 1988), *The Lust Killer* (about Jerome Brudos; Stack, 1983), *Nurses Who Kill* (about numerous male and female nurses who have serially murdered; Linedecker & Burt, 1990), *The Search for the Green River Killer* (Smith & Gullen, 1991), and others. These books contain graphic details of the murders of victims and in some cases list ranges of victims from 3 to more than 50. Readers should note, however, that it would be a mistake to accept all the data found in such books as scientific truth. There are gross errors in more than a few of these paperbacks. For example, in one new book, the author states that Lucas is serving two life sentences in Texas; Lucas is actually under a death sentence. In another book, the author talks about the John Gacy case and makes several factual errors. In the same book the author mentions Bundy being in prison in California, not Florida.

Even the cases reported in careful scientific research can be seriously flawed, if for no other reason than that there are untold numbers of not only victims but serial killers themselves. Our own experience bears this out. In lecturing throughout the United States concerning homicide in general and serial murder in particular, we are continually approached by police officers who discuss cases that they are currently investigating. More often than not, these are cases of suspected serial murder. Recently, while in Ft. Lauderdale, Florida, lecturing at a two-week homicide investigation course, the first author spoke with an officer who was working on a serial murder case that occurred in Gainesville (five young persons murdered, four young women and one man). This was only one of three cases that this officer was involved with that he believed were the work of a serial murderer. This is a typical story.

Many have attempted to make educated estimates regarding the number of serial killers currently murdering in North America. The U.S. Department of Justice at one time estimated that as many as 35 serial killers were roaming the streets and towns of the United States (cited in Reynolds, 1990). Our own research indicates that this is probably a very low estimate. Ted Bundy, in an interview with the first author conducted while Bundy was on death row in Florida, stated that it was his feeling that there were at least 100 serial murderers at large in the United States. Even this number may be too small. From our contacts with law enforcement officials all over the United States, we believe that a more accurate estimate may be as high as 200. It should be remembered that most of these killers are not involved in the murder of scores of people every year. As Bundy said in the interview, "The good [successful] serial killer will only kill two or three people a year unless he gets too greedy." A serial killer who murders too many persons in too short a period of time, especially if the murders are committed in a relatively small geographic area, is more likely to be caught than one who spaces out his murders over time and geography.

As the preceding indicates, there is no empirically proven method for gauging the exact number of serial murderers in the United States today. The lower end of the estimate is 35, but there may be as many as 300 persons who are *actively* involved in the killing of multiple victims each year. This is a figure that will alarm many, and it may cause others to launch accusations of sensationalism. This is not our purpose, however; rather, we are concerned with educating the public as to the extent of this grave problem.

In our interviews with serial murderers already in prison, we are often told, by these convicts, of other inmates who are in prison for rape, burglary, or other criminal acts who have admitted to our interviewees that they are serial murderers. For various reasons, the serial nature of their crimes has gone unnoticed, and many of the murders they have committed have gone unsolved.

The Number of Victims

Just as it is impossible to gauge the number of serial killers accurately, it is equally impossible to give an exact number of victims who fall prey to these serialists. Bernick and Spangler (1985) estimate 5,000 victims a year, a number that many experts reject as not only inaccurate but sensationalistic. However, this figure may indeed by accurate. Bernick and Spangler base their estimate on interviews with experts and extrapolation. How accurate any estimate may be is impossible to measure.

There are hazards to judging the seriousness of serial murder simply in terms of the number of victims one serial murder kills or even the total number of victims of all known or suspected serial killers. In this type of homicide, as in other cases of violent crime, there are also "secondary victims"—the families, friends, and acquaintances of the victims. These huge numbers of secondary victims are never measured. The victimization of parents, spouses, and others close to victims can continue long after the

> "A large number of serial killings [are] an attempt to silence the victims, an extreme but simple form of elimination."
>
> Ted Bundy, interview, April 18, 1987

murder itself. For example, the father of Laura Aime, one of Ted Bundy's victims, was hospitalized for depression after her murder. On one occasion, while he and Jim Massie, a Kentucky parole officer, were driving through the mountain parkway where Laura's body was found, he said, "My little baby was up there by herself and there was nothing I could do to help her." Aime died in 1987 of heart problems, no doubt complicated by the stress of his daughter's death (James Massie, personal communication, August 17, 1989).

Unlike with some other kinds of murder, the families and other survivors of serial murder victims are often exposed to unwanted publicity and exploitation. A mother of one serial killer's victim was so upset by a book written about the serial killer and what the author said about the killing of her daughter that she was hospitalized for a week. She told James Massie that the book's author had never interviewed her about her daughter, a point about which she was quite bitter. She was additionally upset that the author had access to police information that she, as the mother of a primary victim, was denied. In an interview in which Massie spoke with both this mother and another mother of a victim of this killer, they disapproved of a book's being written concerning the murder of their daughters. She was somewhat unnerved that an author could profit from such a crime, a fact that actually contributed to her grief as a secondary victim. She also suffered further because of hearing from others what her daughter suffered before her death. She stated that she had not read the book, and ended the interview by asking, "Why do people write things like this?" (James Massie, personal communication, August 17, 1989).

SPATIAL MOBILITY
AND MALE SERIAL KILLERS

One of the elements used in defining types of serial killers is their spatial mobility or stability. Some serial murderers move from one area to the next, killing in each area. Ted Bundy, for example, killed in several states, including Washington, Oregon, Idaho, Colorado, Utah, and Florida. He may also have killed in California, Iowa, Pennsylvania, and Vermont, as law enforcement officers suspect. Bundy would be classified as a *geographically transient* serial murderer. These nomadic murderers are involved in the killing of persons while they travel from one area to another. They may cruise for thousands of miles each year. Although many experts believe that nomadic serial killers drive thousands of miles in their quest for victims, we have gathered a different picture from our interviews with convicted killers. Those we have talked with indicate that they never lacked for readily available victims within their own neighborhoods; their more rational explanation for their travel is that it was used to confuse police.

There are also *geographically stable* serial murderers. (It must be emphasized that the *stable* in this label has nothing to do with the personality of the killer; it refers here only to spatial mobility.) These killers do not feel comfortable leaving familiar areas in their trolling for victims. Often selecting victims close to their homes or workplaces, geographically stable serialists are more likely to be arrested than are transient killers.

PHASES IN SERIAL MURDER

Several researchers have proposed models of the phases involved in serial murder (Hickey, 1991; Norris, 1988; Rule, 1983, 1988; Stack, 1983), but there is one five-phase model that appears to be most accurate (see Figure 6.1). Not all phases of this model are present in every case; the number of phases varies, not only from one serialist to the next, but, in some cases (e.g., in those committed by an organized killer), from one killing to another.

In all cases of serial killing there is a fantasy, whether sexual, acquisitive, or demonic. This is an integral part of the killing

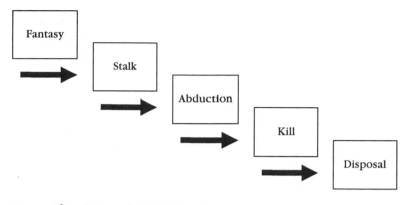

Figure 6.1. Phases in Serial Murder

process. In other words, there must be some idea, thought pattern, or even sexual fantasy that propels the killer into the murderous process. This fantasy is in some cases very simple and in others quite complex—but there is always a fantasy. Typically a serial murderer's fantasy will mirror the needs, motivations, and anticipated gains of the kill. One serial killer we interviewed, for example, had a fantasy that he had incorporated as a script from a cache of pornography he found in his father's garage when he was a child.

The second phase is the stalking of the victim. As with the fantasy, the complexity of the stalk varies with time, opportunity, and the killer's compulsivity. The killer will pursue a victim according to his or her personality as well as the organization of the crime scene itself. In one case that we know of, a killer placed inexpensive watches where he knew the tires of his intended victim's husband's car would run over them, both in the driveway at her home and at the husband's workplace parking lot, to determine what time the husband left home and what time he left work. When the killer attacked the woman, he told her he knew the window of time he had for what he wanted to do. This stalk was complex. The stalk of the more disorganized offender, on the other hand, is typically very simple. Usually such killers just use a sudden attack, and the stalk is almost nonexistent.

More than one of the serialists we interviewed remarked that depersonalization of the victim occurs during the stalking phase.

One man stated that when he started the stalk the victim became an object; as far as he was concerned, she had no husband, no brother or sister, no relatives, friends, or acquaintances. While we talked, this man was holding a paper cup, which he crushed as he spoke. He said he gave no more thought to the crushing of a human life than he gave to the destruction of that cup.

The third phase in serial murder is the abduction. Not all cases of serial murder include an abduction; a disorganized offender, for example, is more likely to carry out a blitz-type attack. In an abduction by an organized offender, there may be some controlled conversation, a verbal ruse, or some other ploy that serves to move the intended victim into the killer's comfort zone for the purpose of the murder. As with other phases in the model, some abductions are very simple and others are quite complex. Further, abductions may vary with time, frequency, and the killer's feeling of compulsion.

The fourth phase is the murder of the selected victim. Holmes and De Burger (1988) describe two types of serial murder acts: act focused and process focused. In the former type, the killing is done swiftly. The important part for this type of killer is the death of the victim; the anticipated gains for this killer are not those of sexual gratification or power. The act is decisive, immediate, and does not depend upon a reaction from the victim. The process-focused killing, on the other hand, is more typical of a lust, thrill, or power/control serialist. This person often has a mental script for the act of murder. There may be certain words to be spoken and certain acts to be performed before the murder can actually occur. Even after the death of the victim, the process-focused kill continues. For example, necrosadistic acts are quite common in this form of murder. Removal of certain parts of the body, especially sexual parts, is the rule more than the exception. The kill ends only when the killer moves into the fifth and final phase of serial murder, the disposal of the corpse.

The disposal of the body may take two forms. The killer may simply leave the site where the murder occurred, leaving the body behind. This kind of action has been linked to the "visionary" and "mission" types of serial killers (Holmes & De Burger, 1985, 1988; see the discussion of typology below). The second form of body disposal is for the killer to move the body after the murder, placing it either so that it will be found or so that it will not. When the first author asked Ted Bundy why he arranged it so that some bodies of his victims were found, he answered with a smile, "To let you know I'm still here" (personal communication, November 17, 1987). In other words, if a serial killer disposes of a body in a location where it will be easily and quickly found, this may be seen as a form of "advertisement."

As we have noted, not all of the five phases discussed above are part of every serial murder. However, consideration of these phases is important because of their usefulness in any investigation of a suspected serial murder case. For instance, if a victim's body has been disposed at a site far removed from the abduction site, and it has also been determined that the victim was murdered at a third location, the investigator can assume that the killer is one who is closer to the organized end than to the disorganized end of the disorganized-organized continuum. The more phases to a serial murder, the more organized the killer may be. The more organized the killer, the more truth to the traits or characteristics of the FBI's typology. For example, if an individual perpetrates a "five-phase" murder, the more likely it is that the killer is intelligent, well educated, living with a sex partner, a police groupie, and so on. These may appear to be small points, but in a serial murder investigation, small points often become part of a synergetic gestalt that leads to a successful resolution of the case.

TYPOLOGY OF MALE SERIAL MURDERERS

There have been only a few attempts to devise a typology of serial murderers based on an analysis of motivations, anticipated gains, and the analysis of the crime scene. For example, Lunde (1976) believes that most mass murderers (a type in which he includes serial murderers) are either paranoid schizophrenics or sexual sadists. A more comprehensive endeavor is the typology offered by Holmes and De Burger (1988). Based on interviews and the analysis of more than 400 cases of serial murder, these researchers identify four types of serial killers: visionary, mission, hedonistic, and power/control. "Each type is labeled in keeping with the kinds and motives that seem to predominate

Typology of Male Serial Murderers

Visionary: The visionary serial killer is impelled to murder because he has heard voices or seen visions demanding that he kill a certain person or category of persons. For some the voice or vision is perceived to be that of a demon; for others it may be perceived as coming from God.

Mission: The mission serial killer has a conscious goal in his life to eliminate a certain identifiable group of people. He does not hear voices or see visions. He has a self-imposed duty to rid the world of a group of people who are "undesirable" or "unworthy" to live with other human beings.

Hedonistic: The hedonistic serial killer kills simply for the thrill of it, because he enjoys it. The thrill becomes an end in itself. The lust murderer can be viewed as a subcategory of this type because of the sexual enjoyment experienced in the homicidal act. Anthropophagy, dismemberment, necrophilia, and other forms of sexual aberration are prevalent in this form of serial killing.

Power/Control: The power or control serial killer receives gratification from the complete control of the victim. This type of murderer experiences pleasure and excitement not from sexual acts carried out on the victim, but from his belief that he has the power to do whatever he wishes to another human being who is completely helpless to stop him.

SOURCE: Holmes and De Burger (1988).

in the killer's homicidal actions. Within each of these types, it is apparent that the motives function to provide the serial killer with a personal rationale or justification for the homicidal violence" (p. 55).

There are other typologies as well, some similar to Holmes and De Burger's and some quite different. For example, Hickey (1991) offers a similar typology but also adds a *place-specific* label to those types of serialists who murder in particular physical locations. Hickey also includes the categories of team killers and solo killers. All three of Hickey's additional types are important to consider in the analysis of serial murder. Levin and Fox (1985) offer "murders of expediency," "murders for profit," and "family slayings."

In addition to the four types of serial murderers already mentioned, the first author has identified a fifth type, the *predator* (Holmes, 1990). This hunter of humans kills not to restore him- or herself to some type of tranquility or state of mental peace, but simply murders continually, with no internal prohibitions to prevent it. This sexual killer has the mind-set of a predator and is constantly "on the hunt." This type of serialist always has the psychological urge to victimize, not to raise himself to a psychological stance of omnipotence, but more as a style of living and, for some, a form of recreation (Holmes, 1990). The first author's interviews with serialists currently in prison have revealed this type of serial killer, who seems to live to effect violence and eventually to kill.

TRAITS OF MALE SERIAL MURDERERS

For an observational and empirical perspective, it is important to examine the various types of serial killers objectively. An examination of the typology offered by Holmes and De Burger (1988) reveals the differing behavioral traits as well as motivational perspectives and perceived gains, material or psychological, of different types of male serial killers (see Table 6.3). For instance, the visionary serial killer selects strangers as his victims, as do all the types of serial murderers outlined by Holmes and De Burger except the comfort killer. The comfort killer, in contrast, typically kills someone he knows for insurance money, business interests, or other types of material gain. The visionary killer is involved in an act-focused killing with little planning. This kind of killer's spatial locations appear to be concentrated. There is little inclination to move the body after the kill because once the murder is committed, the deed is done. Compare this with the traits of lust and power/control killers, who not only commit acts of necrophilia but may keep a body long after the person is dead.

Lust, thrill, and power/control murderers are all process focused. For these types of killers there are psychological gains to be realized from prolonging the act of the murder. This is not a part of the plan, if any plan exists, for visionary and mission killers. The mission killer also shares another trait with the

TABLE 6.3
Homicidal Behavioral Patterns of Male Serial Killers

Factors	Visionary	Mission	Lust	Thrill	Comfort	Power
Victim selection						
specific		X	X	X	X	X
nonspecific	X					
random	X		X	X		X
nonrandom		X			X	
affiliative					X	
strangers	X	X	X	X		X
Methods						
act focused	X	X				
process focused			X	X	X	X
planned		X	X	X	X	X
spontaneous	X					
organized		X	X	X	X	X
disorganized	X					
Spatial locations						
concentrated	X	X				
nomadic			X	X	X	X

visionary killer: His murders tend to be concentrated in one area, although in a wider circle than with the visionary killer.

Clearly, there are wide differences among the various types of men who are fatal serialists. These differences have important implications, not only for researchers but also for law enforcement professionals.

MOTIVATIONAL FACTORS

There are obvious differences in the motivations and anticipated gains in different serial killings. For some, the motivation may stem from a perceived demon or the voice of God. For others, it may be an intense craving found within the psyche of the killer. Some killers have described that feeling to us in interviews, even giving the sensation a name. Some call it "the beast," some "the shadow"; Ted Bundy called it "the entity" (personal communication, November 17, 1987). The focus of this section is an analysis of the various factors at work in the commission of serial murder.

Basic Sources

The behavior of serial murders is usually tied to one of three explanations. Stereotypically, serial killers are viewed as madmen or maniacs, people who may appear strange or bizarre. Although such killers may sometimes look like crazed homicidal maniacs, only rarely can biogenic explanations account for their behavior. As a rule, serial murder cannot be explained by brain waves, blows to the head received in childhood (contrary to the position taken by Norris, 1988), or defective genes in the killer. Levin and Fox (1985) are quite specific in their denunciation of this simplistic charge. The sociogenic approach, which includes theories of learned behavior and cultural violence, certainly has some input into the violent personality and its propensity, perhaps, for serial murder. But sociogenic explanations cannot account directly for the etiology of the serial murderer in particular. The FBI found in a study of the sexually criminal population that many of these criminals possess characteristics that actually are viewed as favorable to socially approved behavior ("The Men Who Murdered," 1985, p. 5). The psychogenic approach also fails to explain the serialist. The "typical" serial murderer is neither insane (a legal term, not a medical one) nor psychotic.

It appears that the serial murderer mind-set arises from a unique combination of traits and experiences, and that the sequence of the each murderer's experiences is so unique that if it had in any way been altered the person likely would *not* have become a serial murderer later in life (Holmes & De Burger, 1985, p. 33).

Location of Motives

What causes serial killers to murder varies not only with location but also with the frequency and duration of the motivation. For example, in an interview with the first author, Ted Bundy said that he did not kill for a period of two years because he was in prison. He then escaped, and within a week he murdered in a fashion not "typical" of his other killings. He had previously murdered in a manner that incorporated all of the five phases described above, however, this time, because the feeling was so strong, and the "entity" that he said made him need to kill was gnawing at his senses, he killed in an especially atypical and brutal fashion. However, when he killed again three weeks after this atypical murder, he killed in a manner very similar to that of the killings he had committed before his initial incarceration. Of course, in this interview Bundy never confessed he did the killings; he only admitted them from a "third-person" position. It was not until shortly before he was executed that he confessed to some of his murders.

The concept of motivation is usually concerned with the question of why a person behaves in a particular manner. In order to understand motivation, one must examine the totality of the individual as well as the source of the motivation. For example, Joseph Kallinger, known as the Shoemaker, launched his killing career with the murder of his son, a neighbor, age 9, and finally a 21-year-old nurse. The motivation for the killing came from an apparition of a disembodied head, which Kallinger called Charlie. Charlie commanded that Kallinger kill everyone in the world and then commit suicide. After his own death, Charlie promised, the Shoemaker would become a god (Schreiber, 1984). The location of Kallinger's motivation thus was psychologically extrinsic. Although a valid argument can be made that Kallinger is insane and there is no Charlie, the end result is the same; the vision and voice were inside the mind of the killer, and the persons in proximity to Kallinger had no knowledge of his intent.

The extrinsic motivation to kill lies outside the personality of the killer. The race-conflict-motivated "Zebra" and "Death Angel" killings are both examples of extrinsic motivation. We include paid assassins and organized crime "hit men" within our definition of serial killers, although some researchers do not, and these killers' motivations also rest outside their own psyches. For such serialists, killing is simply a duty or part of their job.

The majority of serial killers' location of motivation may be considered intrinsic. The very existence of these motives is almost always unknown to others. Even intimates of the serial murderer are seldom aware of the homicidal motives harbored in the mind of a lover, spouse, family member, or close friend. Thus the surviving daughter of Nannie Doss, having had what she viewed as a close relationship with her mother, was shocked and astounded to learn that "mom" had serially murdered 11 people, including two of Mrs. Doss's own children (Holmes & De Burger, 1985, p. 50; Nash, 1980, p. 285).

Behavioral Orientation

It is useful to try to understand what a given killer has to gain from the commission of a particular crime. A serial killer's anticipated gains can be either material or psychological, although in our own research on scores of cases of serial murder, we have found that the preponderance of serialists kill for psychological reasons. In interviews, many have told us that the principal motivating factor in their killing was that they simply enjoyed killing. Others have stated that they were motivated by the intense feelings they got out of holding the fate of other persons in their hands. The more often such a person kills, the greater becomes his need to experience those feelings of gratification or power. The feeling becomes more than a compulsion, it becomes an addiction. And, as with most addictions, there is a need to do more and more to realize the same sense of gratification that less activity could provide in the past.

The accompanying sense of fantasy involved in the commission of most serial murders is further evidence that they are perpetrated for psychological gain. These fantasies often take twisted and often sadistic forms: "Much of the motive and intent in the form of fantasies are vague and loosely formulated until the murderers actually kill. With the reality of the murder, the fantasy feeds off itself and becomes more structured. As more murders are committed, the phases of the murders become more organized" (Holmes, 1989, p. 55).

FEMALE SERIAL MURDERERS

Despite the claims of some researchers (e.g., Reynolds, 1990), there is evidence that some serial killers are female. One reason for the reluctance to accept women as serial killers may be an aversion to the idea that women are capable of this kind of violence. Men, on the other hand, have long been judged as violent persons quite capable of such acts. Traditionally, it has been assumed that women do not kill for sexual reasons, and that women do not kill in response to the voice of God or the devil (Holmes, 1990). Women have historically been viewed as nurturing and vulnerable, not physically or psychologically capable of murder unless provoked in an abusive situation. Reality, however, betrays tradition.

It does appear to be true that most women who kill do so in response to some abusive situation (Goetting, 1989). Some kill because continued abuse has rendered them incapable of seeing any other way out of a bad situation, such as a brutal marriage (Walker, 1984). Other women kill because they have been spurned in love, and they perceive fatal violence to be a just response. The preponderance of women who kill murder because of ill-fated personal relationships. The typical female murderer not only kills someone she knows but also kills inside her own home (Goetting, 1989). Her methods and motivations differ fundamentally from those of the "typical" male murderer. Usually, women who kill for these kinds of reasons do not become involved in serial murder.

Some women may kill because of their involvement in cults or "disciple" relationships. The women in the Manson Family—Leslie Van Houten, Lynette Fromme, and others—are examples of this type. Charlene Gallego, the common-law wife of serial killer Gerald Gallego, aided in his selection and abduction of at least 10 young people (van Hoffman, 1990). Her exact motivations are unknown; she may have been frightened into becoming an accomplice or she may have been willing, enjoying her role.

Hickey (1991), who studied 34 female serial killers, found that 82% of these cases had occurred since 1900. Also, he discovered that almost half of the women had male accomplices. Perhaps one of Hickey's most interesting findings is that more than one in three of the women began their killing careers after 1970. He offers several explanations for this apparent increase: improved police investigation (and thus more knowledge about such cases in general), population increase, and increased media attention. The average woman killed for 9.2 years before her killing stopped, for whatever reason. Most of the women in Hickey's sample were homemakers (32%) or nurses (18%); 15%

were involved in other types of criminal careers when they became killers. One in five of these women killers reported no occupation. Almost all the women (97%) were white; the average age was 33. One-third of Hickey's sample reported having killed strangers (a much lower proportion than among male serial killers), and, almost without exception, the women did not travel in quest of victims. Most of these women killed for material gain, often using poisons or pills (pp. 107-118).

An increasing number of women murder multiple victims. If one uses the definition of three or more victims over more than 30 days (Holmes & De Burger, 1985), several women who can be classified as serialists come immediately to mind. Belle Gunness murdered an estimated 14 to 49 husbands and suitors in LaPorte, Indiana (Langlois, 1985). Nannie Doss murdered 11 husbands and family members in Tulsa (Hickey, 1991). Martha Beck and her lover, Ray Fernandez, stalked and murdered as many as 20 women.

Carol Bundy (no relation to Ted Bundy) serves as an excellent example of a female serial murderer. In the early 1980s, she and Douglas Clark allegedly launched a campaign of lust murder in Los Angeles with the decapitation of Bundy's former lover, Jack Murray, and several young female runaways. She is in prison only for the murder of Murray and one female; Douglas is on death row in California for the murder of six young women. Clark denies involvement in any murders (Farr, 1992, p. 302). Bundy admits to the murder of one woman and Murray (Hickey, 1991, p. 182).

Often women serialists kill for "comfort" purposes: money, insurance benefits, or business interests. Dorothea Puente of Sacramento County, California, was charged with nine murders of elderly roomers who lived in her boardinghouse. She allegedly collected and cashed her victims' social security checks after their murders, a scenario that has been repeated often (Blackburn, 1990).

There are, however, female serialists who kill for other than comfort considerations. Sex, revenge, and love all emerge as intrinsic motivations for homicide. The anticipated gains and the locations of motivation vary from one woman to another. It is this foundation of anticipated gain, location of motivation, spatial mobility, and method of murder that serves as the basis for the following examination and categorization.

SPATIAL MOBILITY
AND FEMALE SERIAL MURDERERS

As discussed earlier in this chapter, there is an initial distinction in serial killers based upon their geographic mobility. Geographically stable killers are those who kill in or near the area in which they live. Most female serial killers are of this type. Carol Bundy and Priscilla Ford are two examples. Bundy lived in Los Angeles and selected victims typically from the area near the intersection of Hollywood and Vine. Priscilla Ford killed her victims in her hometown of Reno, Nevada. Her victims were simply unfortunate persons who happened to be nearby when God demanded that Ford slay them. Few women fall into the category of the geographically transient killer, who travels continually throughout a killing career (Holmes & De Burger, 1985, pp. 30-31). The difference between male and female serial killers in geographic mobility may be in part an artifact of the traditional female role, which center on the home and family. Additionally, women typically are not as occupationally mobile as their male counterparts, and this too may influence their spatial mobility. These elements influence the victim selection process.

As noted above, the geographically stable serial murderer is more likely than the transient serialist to be caught. This is true not only because the killer remains in the community, with personal, occupational, and social ties, but because it means that typically one or at most very few law enforcement agencies are involved, so that turf issues among investigators do not necessarily emerge as detrimental and communication among investigators is not hampered.

Few women are transient in their killings, although there have been some. Christine Gallego is an example. She and her common-law husband murdered in California and Nevada. The geographically transient female serial killer presents problems much like those presented by her male counterpart. The mobility of the killer in itself makes apprehension difficult, and this is complicated by turf issues and lack of communication among involved law enforcement agencies.

TYPOLOGY OF FEMALE SERIAL MURDERERS

From an examination of women who have killed more than three victims in a period of more than 30 days, there emerge several types of female serialists. We call these the visionary, the comfort killer, the hedonistic killer, the power seeker, and the disciple killer.

The Visionary

Most serial killers are not psychotic and are indeed in touch with reality. They have no feelings about the concern and welfare of others; most, perhaps, are psychopaths. By contrast, there are some who commit acts of homicide because they are psychologically extrinsically compelled to murder. These killers may see visions that demand they kill others, perhaps even everyone in the world.

In this type of homicide, the perpetrator has a severe break with reality. This break can be demonstrated by the person's admission that she has spoken to God, an angel, a spirit, or Satan himself. The motivation is extrinsic to the personality and comes from an apparition or an auditory hallucination. In this type of murder, attack is spontaneous. The killer selects a victim based on a description furnished by the message giver.

Priscilla Ford can be classified as a visionary serial killer. She claimed to hear the voice of God as she walked down the streets of Reno, Nevada. The voice demanded that she kill people she met walking on the street. They were "bad people" and deserved to die. The defense of insanity was insufficient to keep her from conviction and death row in Nevada (E. Hickey, personal communication, June 30, 1991).

Another visionary serial murderer was Martha Wise. A 40-year-old widow living in Medina, Ohio, she killed her family members for revenge. She used arsenic to poison her mother after the woman ridiculed Martha for being involved romantically with a man younger than herself. She later fed arsenic to her aunt and uncle. She bungled an attempt to liquidate the rest of her aunt's family by administering a nonlethal amount of arsenic. Wise claimed that the devil had followed her everywhere and forced her to commit the killings (E. Hickey, personal communication, June 30, 1991).

Typology of Female Serial Murderers

Visionary: The visionary serial killer is impelled to murder because she has heard voices or seen visions demanding that she kill a certain person or category of persons. For some the voice or vision is perceived to be that of a demon; for others it may be perceived as coming from God.

Comfort: The comfort serial killer murders for money, for instance, from insurance or from business interests. She kills for material, not psychological, gain. She typically kills persons she knows, such as husbands, her children, suitors, or roomers.

Hedonistic: The hedonistic serial killer is perhaps the least understood of all female serial killers. The hedonistic killer has made a vital connection between sexual gratification and fatal violence. She kills for psychological gain, typically for sexual purposes.

Power seeker: The power-seeking serial killer murders in order to attain some perceived form of power. Nurses who deliberately put their patients at risk so that they can rush in at the last moment and save them are examples of this type. Typically, nurses involved in these acts eventually tire of the charade, kill whatever patient they have been using, and move on to another.

Disciple: The disciple killer has fallen under the spell of a charismatic leader and kills upon command. The killer's motivation comes from outside, from the leader, and her psychological gain comes from pleasing the leader by doing his bidding.

For the visionary killer, an insanity plea can be effective. This person is mentally ill. However, it must be noted that some individuals may claim to see visions or hear voices in an attempt to be found insane and thus escape severe punishment. David Berkowitz, for example, stated that his neighbor's dog commanded him to kill. He later recanted this story.

The Comfort Killer

Most female serial killers are of the comfort type. Their motivation is material, rather than psychological, gain. The motivation is internal to the killer's psyche. There are no voices or visions from God or the devil demanding a murder.

The comfort serial killer typically murders persons with whom she is acquainted in order to gain money—through insurance benefits, inheritance of business interests, or whatever. Such killers are not always female, of course. Around the turn of the century, one man, H. H. Mudgett in Chicago, may have killed as many as 200 people for insurance and business payoffs (Eckert, 1985).

In 1901, Amy Archer-Gilligan opened a rest home in Connecticut. During the next 14 years she disposed of at least 27 men and women by poison. Of the men she nursed, she married 5, insured them for substantial amounts of money, and then promptly killed them. Amy also killed women after convincing them to let her assist them in rewriting their wills. She died in a mental facility in 1928 (E. Hickey, personal communication, July 12, 1991).

Anna Hahn, a native of Germany, moved to Cincinnati in 1929. She volunteered to serve as a nurse for several elderly men she had met at various beer gardens. The men strangely started dying, even though Hahn "provided constant care." She called herself an "angel of mercy," but was found guilty of several cases of murder. She was executed in May 1938 (E. Hickey, personal communication, July 12, 1991).

Janice Gibbs, a grandmother, killed her husband, three sons, and an infant grandson for $31,000 in insurance money. A native of Georgia, she was given five consecutive life sentences in 1976 (E. Hickey, personal communication, July 12, 1991).

Mary Eleanor Smith trained her son in the "art of killing," teaching him to rob men and then dump the bodies in muriatic acid beneath their home in Montana. Found guilty of multiple counts of murder, she was given a life sentence in 1920 (E. Hickey, personal communication, July 12, 1991).

Dorothea Puente in Sacramento County, California, was charged in 1988 with nine counts of murder after the authorities found bodies in the side yard of her rooming house. She allegedly killed her roomers for their social security checks. Earlier in her criminal career, she had been convicted of forgery in attempting to cash 34 checks belonging to tenants (E. Hickey, personal communication, July 12, 1991).

The Hedonistic Killer

Perhaps the least understood and least represented among female serial killers is the hedonistic type. Hedonism is the doctrine that pleasure is the highest good. The hedonistic serial killer is one who has made a vital connection between fatal violence and sexual gratification.

Carol Bundy is currently at the California Institution for Women at Frontera. She is serving consecutive sentences of 25 years to life and 27 years to life for the murder of her former boyfriend, former manager of the apartment complex where she and Douglas Clark, known as the Hollywood Strip Killer, lived, and for the murder of a prostitute. Bundy was allegedly involved not only in the killing of Murray but in the murders of several young women who were runaways and prostitutes. Clark has said that Bundy killed young women and decapitated them. She allegedly placed the heads in her refrigerator so that she could later retrieve them and use them in aberrant sex acts. The sexual life-style of Carol Bundy, which included the murder of her victims, would certainly place her in the category of hedonistic killer. Her anticipated gain appeared to be psychological: personal and sexual pleasure. Her motivation was intrinsic to her personality; apparently there were no voices or visions that impelled her to murder. Bundy did not rob the victims; no money, jewelry, or personal articles were taken. It must be noted here that Bundy denies any responsibility for the murders of the young women claimed to be victims of Bundy and Clark. Clark claims that Bundy was the killer of the young women (Farr, 1992; Hickey, 1991, pp. 181-182). If indeed Bundy was intimately involved in these series of killings, she would be classified as a geographically stable serial murderer, hedonistic type.

The Power Seeker

Power is the ability to influence the behavior of others in accordance with one's own desires. Power has status in any society. Women who are classified as power-seeking serial killers are those who murder as a way to attain a sense of power. The motivations and anticipated gains of these killers are very different from those of other types of serial murderers.

One power-seeking female serial murderer is Jane Toppan, who was a nurse. Authorities noted that two of her patients died quite mysteriously. After an investigation, she was discovered to have murdered as many as 100 victims. She proudly explained that she had fooled the authorities, "the stupid doctors," and "the ignorant relatives" for years before her discovery (Hickey, 1991). Such killers often will poison their victims and "come to their rescue" time and time again to prove their life-saving skills (Hickey, 1991, pp. 221, 225; also personal communication, June 30, 1991). Typically, this kind of killer will tire of this charade, kill the patient, and move on to another.

Genene Jones, a pediatric nurse in San Antonio, Texas, was arrested for the murder of young children who had been admitted to hospitals often for very minor medical problems. Thought to be responsible for as many as 16 deaths of infants (Elkind, 1989, p. 392), this serialist felt important in the hospital setting as a primary medical caretaker. The motivations of power-seeking serial killers appear to be similar to those found in people with a little-known psychological condition called "Munchausen syndrome by proxy," which has been receiving some attention lately in the media. Individuals who have this disorder have been known to fabricate and/or to induce medical problems in children under their care, including their own children. Power-seeking serial killers apparently are motivated by their own self-perceptions of worthlessness to create life-and-death situations in which they can be heroes and thus gain feelings of importance. Jones seems to be such a personality. Her behavior in harming children was akin to that of "the volunteer fireman who sets a blaze, then appears first at the scene in hope of becoming a hero" (Elkind, 1989).

The motivation of the power seeker is clearly intrinsic; the psyche of the killer demands satisfaction. Satisfaction for this killer does not come from the act of killing itself, but from being perceived as the one responsible for averting a death; the rewards come in the form of adulation, from others on the scene as well as from relatives of the patient who almost died.

The Disciple Killer

Some women, like some men, kill because they are under influence of a charismatic leader. Immediately several cases come to mind, the most infamous being those of the women involved with Charles Manson. Lynette Fromme, Leslie Van Houten, and the other women in the Manson Family committed unspeakable acts of violence because they wanted to please Manson.

The motivation for this type of female serial murderer is linked to a source outside the psyche, the charismatic leader. Jim Jones is an example of such a leader. Despite various problems in his final days, including financial difficulties and illness, Jones was able to influence many of his followers to do whatever he wished, up to and including committing suicide. The gain for the disciple killer is psychological; she hopes to be accepted by her idol. Victim selection is typically arranged by the leader. For example, Manson allegedly selected the homes to which he sent his disciple killers.

Although the Manson Family murders are perhaps the most famous example of disciple-type killing, there have been other cases as well. In 1982, Judy Neeley and her much older husband, Alvin, were involved in forgeries, burglaries, and robberies. The couple eventually began to abduct, abuse, rape, and murder their victims. Judy claimed that her husband forced her to commit torture and murder because she was completely dominated by him. While in Alabama, they abducted a 13-year-old girl and held her captive for several days. Judy watched while Alvin raped the girl on four occasions, and while he tortured and abused the child. Finally, Judy injected Drano into the girl's veins, but when that failed to kill, she shot her victim in the back and pushed her over a cliff. The Neeleys later abducted a husband and a wife. They marched the couple into a wooded area and shot them both. The man survived the shooting and later testified against the Neeleys. They were arrested, tried, and convicted, and they are now on death row in Alabama. The final number of their victims was never determined (E. Hickey, personal communication, July 28, 1991).

Charlene Gallego married her husband, Gerald, not knowing he was still legally married to another. Unlike her husband,

Charlene grew up in a home where love and affection were freely shown. Soon after her involvement with Gerald began, however, she accepted his life-style, including his bizarre sexual fantasies. She would solicit young women for Gerald by promising them employment, and then would drive them around in a van while Gerald raped them. She then drove them to the places where Gerald would kill them and dispose of their bodies. Involved in the killings of at least nine young women and one young man, Charlene finally turned state's evidence and is currently in prison in Nevada, serving two concurrent sentences of 16 years (Blackburn, 1990).

Martha Beck and her lover, Ray Fernandez, advertised in "lonely hearts" magazines for female companionship. The women who answered these ads quickly became victims. They were strangled, battered, drowned, poisoned, or shot to death. To demonstrate her affection for her lover, once, after drowning a 2-year-old child in a bathtub, while her hands still held the dead girl under water, Beck summoned Fernandez, gleefully exclaiming, "Oh, come and look what I've done, sweetheart." A reliable estimate of the number of women killed by Beck and Fernandez is 20. Arrested in Michigan and sent to New York to stand trial for murders committed there, both were electrocuted in Sing Sing in 1951 (E. Hickey, personal communication, July 17, 1991).

A strange personal chemistry appears to exist in some relationships that results in series of murders that probably would not have occurred had not the two parties met. This same statement can be made of some other types of serial murderers as well, such as in the case of Carol Bundy and Douglas Clark. Neither killed before they shared their common fantasy. This was also the case for Angelo Buono and Kenneth Bianchi, the Hillside Stranglers. This chemistry was also evident between Alton Coleman and Debra Brown. Brown lived with the abusive Coleman; violence became a part of their relationship and savagery became an integral part of their killing. Brown followed Coleman's lead when she killed an elderly couple in Cincinnati using a four-foot wooden candlestick, a crowbar, vice-grip pliers, and a knife. She is thought to have killed as many as eight persons in the company of Coleman. She received two death sentences, life in prison, and a dozen additional years. Even after her trial and incarceration, Brown remained loyal to her lover and signed legal documents making the two common-law partners (Hickey, 1991, pp. 179-180).

TRAITS OF TYPES
OF FEMALE SERIAL KILLERS

The distinctions among types of female serial killers discussed above may be refined and categorized into definitive traits. Knowledge about these traits can lead to better understanding and increased apprehension of female serial killers. The behavioral traits of different kinds of female serial murderers are discussed in this section. This examination centers on victim selection, methods, and spatial locations of murders. Table 6.4 shows these factors and how they apply for each of the five types of female serial killers that have been developed in this chapter. For example, the visionary serial killer typically will attack nonspecific victims. This killer chooses victims randomly and typically kills strangers. Among women serialists, only comfort murderers normally kill people they know—husbands, suitors, children, and so on. Disciple killers murder victims preselected by their leaders; these killers are not involved in determining their victims' suitability for assault.

Methods of murder also vary with the type of female serialist. For instance, only the visionary kills spontaneously. Comfort murderers are act-focused killers; they kill because of anticipated material gain, and the process of killing is not itself the important part. Hedonistic killers, on the other hand, are process focused—these killers murder for the pleasure they get out of the killing itself. The crime scene of the visionary killer is typically disorganized, whereas those of the other kinds of killers are organized. Finally, hedonistic and power-seeking killers often dispose of the bodies of their victims somewhere distant from the places where the crimes occurred.

The spatial mobility of female serial killers varies as well. For example, vision and comfort types tend to kill within the areas in which they live. The other three types are more nomadic in their crimes, not unlike the lust, thrill, and power/control types among male serial murderers (Holmes & De Burger, 1988).

TABLE 6.4
Homicidal Behavioral Patterns of Female Serial Killers

Factors	Visionary	Comfort	Hedonistic	Disciple	Power
Victim selection					
specific		X	X		X
nonspecific	X			X	
random	X		X		
nonrandom		X		X	X
affiliative		X			
strangers	X		X	X	X
Methods					
act focused	X			X	X
process focused		X	X		
planned		X	X	X	X
spontaneous	X				
organized		X	X	X	X
disorganized	X				
Spatial locations					
concentrated	X	X			
nomadic			X	X	X

CONCLUSION

Serial murder has become a serious problem in the United States. With increased media coverage of this type of crime, more and more citizens are becoming aware of their personal vulnerability and possible victimization. Serial killers are indeed a threat throughout North America. Canada, for example, has had its share of serial murderers; Clifford Olsen immediately comes to mind.

Although until recently many researchers and law enforcement personnel believed that all serial killers are men, there are indications that an increasing number of women are involved in serial homicide. Priscilla Ford, Charlene Gallego, Velma Barfield, and others are examples of an emerging number of women serialists who pose grave danger. Women still represent only a very small percentage of all cases of serial murder, but this does not negate the potential danger such women pose to society. The character of the female serial killer is also changing. As

Hickey (1991) notes: "Over the past few years, female offenders killed fewer family members . . . while increasingly targeting strangers. . . . Those who had male partners were much more likely to use violence in killing their victims" (p. 127).

Clearly, no single motivation can account for the murderous acts of either males or females. For example, indications suggest that many women kill for financial (material) gain, but the literature suggests more complex explanations, often bordering on sociopathy or psychopathy (Egger, 1990; Hickey, 1991; Holmes, 1989).

Most research into serial murder has concentrated on male offenders. Because there are distinct differences between male and female serial killers, and because the danger to society from women serialists appears to be increasing, more research needs to be devoted to furthering our understanding of the women who commit such crimes. However, the male serial killer still presents the greatest danger to vulnerable persons, especially women and children.

7

Terrorism and Homicide

Since 1970, terrorism has become a perceived major threat to the world. The expected gains of terrorist groups vary, as do their motives and patterns of operation. Some terrorist activities are well planned and some are not; some are motivated by political or religious ideology, and some simply by money (Merkl, 1986). Others are the result of personal psychopathology. Yet, until approximately the mid-1980s, the U.S. response to the threat of terrorism was mostly lethargic, except for reactive rhetoric to specific incidents.

The incidence of terrorist acts has dramatically escalated worldwide since the early 1970s, especially within the Western nations. In North America, however, terrorism has considerably diminished, although North Americans have not remained completely free of terrorist violence. For example, 40% of all deaths caused by terrorism have involved Americans and Canadians, but not necessarily within the boundaries of either country (Kerstetter, 1983, p. 1529). But these are not all the acts that result in killings.

Terrorist acts such as bombings, setting of fires, and assassinations are typically specific in their targets; that is, the selection of victims is deliberate. However, often persons other than those targeted are harmed; for example, when terrorists carry out a skyjacking they may have a specific target, but all of that airplane's passengers are affected. The terrorist's aim is to demoralize the enemy, and the potential for harm to innocent persons is related to this goal; terrorists hope by their actions to render the enemy restless, uncertain, and ineffective (Weinberg & Davis, 1989).

INCIDENCE OF TERRORISM

For purposes of this discussion, *terrorism* is defined as premeditated, politically motivated violence, perpetrated against noncombatant targets by subnational groups or clandestine state agents, usually to influence an audience. More cumbersome definitions offered by the U.S. Department of Defense, the FBI, the State Department, the Department of Justice, and the Vice President's Task Force on Combating Terrorism (1986) include all the following elements: (a) the unlawful use of force or violence by revolutionary organizations, (b) the intention of coercion or intimidation by governments for political or ideological purposes, (c) premeditated political violence perpetrated against noncombatant targets by subnational groups or clandestine state agents, and (d) use of assassination or kidnapping (U.S. Department of Justice, 1988, p. viii).

Terrorist acts differ according to the anticipated gains of the groups perpetrating them, and the behavioral patterns of different terrorist organizations vary as well. Further, the reasons for the increase in terrorism over the past decades may be separate from the religious and political ideologies that stimulate terrorist activity. For example, accessibility of long-distance transportation has greatly increased since the 1960s. The availability of relatively inexpensive jet travel makes it possible for a person to travel great distances in only a small portion of a day. Air transportation not only affords almost instant mobility, it also provides the terrorist with an opportunity to take action.

Communication is another aspect of modern society that enables the terrorist to become a visible agent to the world. The electronic news media have given terrorists an immediate audience. For example, in February 1974, Patty Hearst was kidnapped in California by a small terrorist group called the Symbionese

Overview of Domestic Terrorist Incidents in the United States,
1980-1986

Target	Percentage
Government buildings and properties	19.9
Commercial establishments	12.5
Diplomatic establishments	6.6
Diplomatic property	2.9
Diplomatic persons	2.9
Military	11.0
Public utilities	5.9
Banks and armored trucks	5.1
Residences	5.1
Transportation facilities	4.4
Educational facilities	3.7
Recreational and entertainment facilities	3.7
Press and media	2.9
Public safety and personnel	2.9
Vehicles	2.2
Persons (other than diplomatic)	2.2
Postal facilities	2.2
Other	3.7

SOURCE: Federal Bureau of Investigation (1986, p. 57).
NOTE: Percentages may not add to 100 because of rounding.

Liberation Army (SLA) (Parry, 1976, p. 352). In the months that
followed, the SLA was given national news attention as the group
killed and plundered before being eliminated in a fiery shoot-out
(Parry, 1976, p. 342). The SLA was responsible for at least 12
deaths of officials and police officers. The group's founder was a
highly regarded black Oakland educator, Dr. Marcus Foster. Ironically, the organization was spawned when the well-intentioned
professor became involved with a therapy group made up of black
prisoners and changed his political views as a result.

INGREDIENTS OF TERRORISM

The rhetoric of all terrorists is strikingly similar. The language
is that of absolutism, of black and white (no shades of gray), "us

versus them," "good versus evil," and so on. However, although there are similarities among terrorists—paranoia is common, for instance—there is no specific or unique mind-set, no striking psychological abnormality. Post (1987), in an article titled "Rewarding Fire With Fire," suggests that terrorist groups tend to attract paranoid personalities and those who seek outside sources to blame for their own inadequacies. According to Post, if there is a distinguishing feature of most terrorists, it is their need to belong and achieve an identity. The terrorist group becomes their family and value system.

In general, the ideology of the terrorist group is highly antiauthority; the group's entire purpose is usually to oppose some form of authority. Within the organization itself, however, the structure is often highly authoritarian. Post (1987) argues that it is possible that this intense ambivalence concerning power and authority explains the patterns of shifting leadership and difficulty in sustaining leadership that are often found in terrorist groups. However, these patterns appear to be more characteristic of European and Latin American terrorist groups than of Middle Eastern organizations (Post, 1987). Perhaps the religious orientation of Middle Eastern groups helps to explain their greater stability. For example, groups such as the Palestine Liberation Organization and the Popular Front for the Liberation of Palestine have experienced continuous leadership over long periods of time (Post, 1987).

For terrorism to be effective it must generate a high level of fear within an intended audience (Cooper, 1982, p. 12). To generate this high level of fear, the terrorist group must be willing to use a substantial amount of force against a specific group for a particular purpose. Of course, the terrorist must be willing to pay a high price for his or her dedication to the activity, even death. An effective terrorist act must also be "cost-effective," and, as a form of nonverbal communication, must get across the ideological message—the philosophy or the point of view it is intended to illustrate.

Nettler (1982) offers the following list of common ingredients in terrorism:

1. *No rules:* Terrorists differ from soldiers in war and police action in that terrorists consciously violate all conventions.

2. *No innocents:* The "unjust system" includes a fight against all people with that system who do not side with them.
3. *Economy:* By a single act of terrorism, the act serves to frighten tens of thousands, or even millions, of people.
4. *Publicity:* Terrorists seek publicity, which in turn encourages terrorism. Well-publicized violence advertises the terrorist's cause.
5. *Individual therapy:* Fighting may be fun to some fanatics to a cause. Engaging in a battle gives purpose to life and all the more to lives that are meaningless.
6. *Varied objectives:* One goal of the terrorist act is to exercise power and to get more of it. However, what power is used for may be variously conceived by the members of the group. (pp. 228-237)

CHARACTERISTICS OF TERRORISTS

Golman (1986) notes that many terrorists share some common social and behavioral experiences. Generally, terrorists tend to be intelligent, industrious, and committed persons; their average age is 22.5 years. Their youth is a factor in their conversion and loyalty to ideological causes. Leadership shifts may redirect their activities, but their fevered commitment to their cause holds steadfast. Many of those involved in terrorist activities have undergone some type of life-threatening experience, such as war or disease, during their formative years. From this experience, they may develop a sense of anomie that causes them to deny the risk of death or any form of personal vulnerability. The terrorist often attaches him- or herself to a political ideology that reflects how he or she views the world. The adopted ideology reflects the needs of the terrorist and fulfills a need within the personality that was formed by past personal experiences (Golman, 1986; Gutteridge, 1986, p. 4).

According to Kerstetter (1983), most terrorists are young, unmarried males who take action in an effort to eradicate injustices in their country. Hasty (quoted in Brody, 1981), although denying Cooper's (1982) contention that terrorists are either criminal or psychopathic, has found that terrorists are usually the youngest child in the family, usually have older brothers, often have a hatred for their fathers, have lost contact with the reality of the world around them, and suffer great feelings of persecution while experiencing feelings of personal grandeur.

A general profile, then, can be developed from the research cited above. The terrorist is most often a young man, in his early 20s, not a criminal, but may be psychotic, who aligns himself with those who shared an early life-threatening experience. Also, as obvious as it is, it is very seldom verbalized—a terrorist is typically gainfully employed and terrorism is only a part-time avocation.

Of course, there are always exceptions to this profile (Rapoport, 1988). For one thing, there are many female terrorists. For instance, women have long been involved in the activities of the Irish Republican Army. Some have been jailed; others have been killed while committing terrorist activities.

Many terrorists profess to follow a "doctrine of necessity" in their activities. That is, they claim to adhere to a philosophy that would, in a just world, oppose the use of violence on principle, but, because of the unjust system in which they find themselves, they believe they are justified in making themselves heard by using the only means available to them, which is violence. Even fatal violence may be justified if there is no other alternative. Once a person accepts this philosophy, he or she can view acts of terrorism as righteous and just (Cooper, 1982).

As we have done with the other types of offenders discussed in this book, we offer below a brief typology of terrorists. The categories are based on work by Hacker (1976), who lists three types of terrorists: criminals, crazies, and crusaders. It should be noted that these labels apply to the motivations of terrorists, and not to the methods they use (although methods may sometimes vary according to motivations).

The first type is the criminal. Hacker acknowledges that few terrorists are truly criminals; that is, few have purely criminal motives. Terrorists for the most part do not commit their violent acts for personal monetary gain; rather, they have ideological gains in mind. Hacker categorizes organized crime operatives as criminal terrorists who are interested in maintaining the status quo. Among criminal-type terrorists, the only terrorist act infrequently seen is hostage taking.

Hacker's second type of terrorist is the "crazy." This kind of terrorist is simply that: probably mentally ill or having serious mental problems. The motivation of this terrorist is not a felt need for political change, but the thrill realized in committing the acts. Clearly this kind of terrorist does not fit the definition we are applying in this chapter; our main concern is with only those terrorists who act out of political or ideological convictions. Hacker places serial murderers in this category; we disagree with this assessment. Hacker's definition of the crazy-type terrorist as one who is not motivated by political gain but by the thrill of committing terrorist acts may appear to fit some serial killers, but, as we have shown in Chapter 6, the serialist's motivations are far more complicated than this simple description would indicate.

The third type of terrorist—the typical type, according to Hacker—is the crusader. This terrorist is motivated by political ideology and believes in the use of violence against noncombatants in a society that can change only if violence is used.

White (1991, p. 112) argues that Hacker's typology of terrorists is simplistic, but we believe it may be useful as a starting point for understanding the types of persons involved in terrorist activities. Such a typology can provide those in law enforcement with some clues as to how to approach certain situations, such as negotiation with hostage takers. This position is reinforced by Bolz (1980, 1984), who believes that successful negotiations with terrorists may start with an analysis of their motivations.

TERRORIST GROUPS

In the United States there are several examples of terrorist groups, some of which are described below.

The Symbionese Liberation Army

One of the most infamous terrorist groups to appear in the United States was the Symbionese Liberation Army, "a small band of self-styled revolutionaries who were among the most wanton remnants of the 1960s" (Gross, 1988, p. C1). The SLA is probably best known for the kidnapping of Patricia Hearst, a member of the powerful Hearst newspaper family, when she

TABLE 7.1

Terrorist Incidents Attributed to Domestic Terrorist Groups in the United States, 1980-1986

Date	Total Incidents[a]	Killed	Injured	Total International Terrorism Subprogram Preventions
1980	13	1	15	—[b]
1981	16	0	3	—[b]
1982	14	2	0	3
1983	11	0	0	2
1984	0	0	0	3
1985	0	0	0	6
1986	0	0	0	3

SOURCE: Federal Bureau of Investigation (1986, p. 60).
a. Represents all incidents attributed to international terrorist groups or individuals.
b. This statistic was not maintained in 1980 or 1981.

was 19 years old and a student at the University of California at Berkeley. After her abduction she became a member of the group and assisted SLA members in several bank robberies and other terrorist activities. Through a process of "brainwashing," the members of the SLA recruited Hearst and converted her to their political goal of overturning society.

After one SLA bank robbery in which she participated, Hearst (then calling herself Tania) was apprehended by the police and was sentenced to prison (Baker & Brompton, 1974; Weed & Swanton, 1976). Today living a normal suburban life, Hearst told a reporter for the *New York Times* in a 1988 interview that she now feels society understands more about the methods and motives of terrorist organizations: "I really feel vindicated finally. They [the SLA] . . . [were] sociopaths on the loose. . . . They raped me mentally, physically, and emotionally and they stole my reputation" (quoted in Gross, 1988, pp. C1, C8).

The membership of the SLA was composed of a mixture of white radical female students from the University of California at Berkeley and black ex-convicts who had served time at the California State Prison in Vacaville. According to Laqueur (1988),

"Counting about a dozen members, it was one of the smallest and most bizarre terrorists groups. . . . it can perhaps be understood against that specific California background which has remained a riddle to most foreigners" (pp. 244-245).

Fueled by a sense of social guilt and a sexual identity crisis (Vetter & Perlstein, 1991, p. 75), they named themselves "Symbionese," which meant to them "a body of harmony of dissimilar bodies and organisms living in deep and loving harmony and partnership in the best interest of the body" (Laqueur, 1988, p. 244). The SLA emblem depicted a seven-headed cobra, signifying God and life, surrounded by slogans against the perceived ills of society (p. 244).

The black males who joined the group were very different from the white female college students. They were reared in deprived areas, typically in Los Angeles, where crime and drug use were commonplace. Surrounded by the values of the white community, but living in deprived circumstances, these individuals developed a sense of hopelessness, or anomie. Their political and paramilitary stance also developed; they became convinced that only through armed confrontation could social change occur. Social ills such as racism could be resolved only through armed conflict and acts of terrorism.

The SLA effectively ceased to be active after a shoot-out with police left six members of the group dead (Vetter & Perlstein, 1991, p. 109). Hearst was subsequently sentenced to prison.

The Weather Underground

The Weather Underground is an example of a terrorist group on the political and ideological left. Most members of this group were white, college-educated, middle-class persons; they were disciplined, well trained, and flexible. These characteristics are some of those that Strentz (1988) lists as profile characteristics of leaders and followers in leftist groups in general; Strentz also notes particular characteristics found in the "opportunists" or "criminal element" in such groups active in the 1960s and 1970s (see the accompanying text box).

The Weather Underground was founded in May 1969 as the result of a meeting of the Students for a Democratic Society in

Profile of 1960s and 1970s Leftist Terrorist Groups

Leader	*Opportunist or Criminal Element*	*Follower*
Male or female	Male	Male or female
No specific race or religion	No specific race or religion	No specific race or religion
College education or attendance	No college	College education or in college
25-40 years old	20-30 years old	20-25 years old
Middle-class	Lower-class	Middle-class
Urban/sophisticated	Urban or rural, with good street sense	Urban/sophisticated
Multilingual	Literate in native language	Multilingual
High verbal skills	High verbal skills	Good verbal kills
Well-trained perfectionist	Learned criminal skills	Well trained
Dedicated	Selfish	Dedicated
Strong personality	Strong personality	Weak personality
Politically active prior to terrorist/ criminal activity	Years of criminal activity; recruited from prison, politics peripheral	Politically active prior to terrorist activity

SOURCE: Strentz (1988).

Chicago. Originally calling themselves the Weathermen, they changed their name to rid themselves of the perceived sexist title. A militant group upon its founding, its mission was expressed thus: "Our intention is to disrupt the empire . . . to incapacitate it, to put pressure on the cracks, to make it hard to carry out its bloody functioning" (quoted in Homer, 1983, p. 149).

In the winter of 1969 the Weather Underground turned into an urban paramilitary organization with the manifest purpose of being the main arm of urban terrorism in the United States. Aiding in the escape of LSD guru Timothy Leary from prison to Algeria, the Weather Underground claimed responsibility for multiple bombings and other acts of terrorism into the mid-1970s. By the end of the 1970s, however, the ideals of the groups were never sufficiently articulated, and the organization failed to realize its goals (White, 1991).

Other Leftist Groups

There are other leftist ideological groups that have risen and fallen, failing to reach their goals of changing the world. The New World Liberation Front attacked major corporations in the United States and operated other terrorist organizations such as the Chicano Liberation Front, the Red Guerrilla Family, and the Black Guerrilla Family (White, 1991, p. 26).

The United Freedom Front (UFF) became a well-known terrorist organization in the mid-1980s. The group's eight members began a series of bombings, killed three police officers, and were finally arrested in Ohio and Virginia. Seven of the members were given long prison sentences for their activities in terrorism (Vetter & Perlstein, 1991, pp. 53-54; White, 1991, pp. 29-30).

Black Leftist Groups

It is not only middle-class, educated whites who appear to have a propensity for joining in terrorist activities. In the 1960s and 1970s especially, blacks served as a catalyst for social action to right perceived social injustices. Some black leftist groups were founded in prisons, where men serving time for property and personal crimes began to think about organizing against the society that they saw as having committed gross injustices against them. They joined forces with other groups who shared their sense of oppression, regardless of race. According to Vetter and Perlstein (1991), one such group, the Black Panthers, "took the position that both blacks and whites were oppressed by the capitalistic system and therefore did not advocate a racist position" (p. 56). As Gurr (1988) notes, the revolutionary rhetoric of such groups is best seen as a gesture of solidarity with those in the Third World, "not a serious threat from a U.S. minority" (p. 561).

There are today some black terrorist groups in operation. The Republic of New Afrika (RNA), for example, was involved in four homicides and numerous armored truck robberies in 1986 and

---

One Month of Terrorism: May 1990

May 1	La Resistencia, a Maoist group, clashed with riot police in Los Angeles.
May 2	Two Mohawk Indians were shot dead in fighting between factions of the Warriors Society in New York State.
May 9	A bomb exploded at a sawmill in Sonoma County, California. Earth First! activists suspected.
May 14	Masked gunmen in camouflage shot and killed four men in a Texas cafe.
May 20	A bomb exploded in the Sheraton Hotel, New York, as a Jewish organization was due to hear a speech by Vice President Dan Quayle.
May 23	A bomb exploded in the New York Hilton as Jeane Kirkpatrick, former U.S. Ambassador to the United Nations, was about to address graduating Jewish college students.
May 24	Two Earth First! activists were injured when a bomb exploded in their car in Oakland, California.

SOURCE: *Terror Update* (No. 15, July 1990, p. 9).

1987. The RNA calls for the creation of an independent black nation in existing southern states, including Alabama, Georgia, Louisiana, Mississippi, and South Carolina. The group also wants the federal government to pay black citizens $10,000 each as recompense for the slavery that all blacks have experienced in this country.

Another militant group with views akin to those of the RNA is the New Afrikan Freedom Fighters. In 1984, several members were arrested in New York City, where they had planned to bomb police cars and kill police officers (Anti-Defamation League of B'nai B'rith, Civil Rights Division, 1988; Vetter & Perlstein, 1991; White, 1991).

Fuqua and the Ahmadiyya Movement in Islam are two other black terrorist groups that have been known to exercise violence in their quest for "social equality" (Vetter & Perlstein, 1991, p. 56). When the El Rukns, a Chicago street gang, were investigated by the local police, they were found to have weapons that included an antitank gun that was sold to them by an unknown underground operation (Vetter & Perlstein, 1991, pp. 56-57).

The Black Liberation Army (BLA) developed as a faction of the Black Panthers. The BLA committed almost 30 acts of terrorism, reaching a peak between 1971 and 1975. These attacks mostly involved police facilities and personnel. Assassination seemed to be the group's preferred form of action; the BLA killed more than 15 police officers in New York, Chicago, Atlanta, San Francisco, and other cities across the United States. Many of the group's members were killed or in prison by 1975. In 1981, some members of the BLA were involved in the robbery of a Brink's armored truck. The influence of this group has decidedly diminished in the past decade (White, 1991, pp. 23, 166).

SINGLE-ISSUE TERRORISTS

Vetter and Perlstein (1991, p. 57) list three types of terrorist groups as examples of single-issue organizations: animal rights groups, prolife (or antiabortion) groups, and groups formed to protest negative treatment of Jews (see also Schmid & De Graaf, 1982). Although we recognize that many single-issue terrorist groups have not yet caused any deaths, the focus of this section is on groups whose propensity for violence may lead to homicide.

Animal Rights Groups

Animal rights activists gained national media attention in 1990 with the arrest of a young woman, Fran Trutt, in Connecticut. Trutt was accused of placing a bomb near the parking space of the owner of a company involved in testing medical equipment on animals. When police searched her apartment, they found a shotgun and other bombs, along with a collection of animal rights literature (Vetter & Perlstein, 1991, p. 63). One group, the Animal Liberation Front, has on occasion claimed responsibility for bombings at medical school labs, animal research labs, and cosmetic companies involved in animal testing. Clearly, the majority of animal rights organizations are not involved in violence, nor do most members desire to express their point of view by violence. Many believe that acts such as Trutt's actually divert attention from their ideological stance of better and more humane treatment for animals.

Prolife Activists

Many prolife activists are waging a terrorist battle against abortion rights. For the most part, prolife groups are acting upon their religious conviction that abortion is murder; some believe that the use of violence is justified in preventing abortion clinics from operating. Antiabortion terrorists committed more than 40 attacks against family planning and abortion clinics in the mid-1980s. There were no reported deaths, but in some cases there were minor injuries that resulted in hospitalization (Hoffman, 1987, pp. 238-239). Not all of these groups' activities involve bombings or shootings. In some cases, prolife activists harass women who are attempting to enter a clinic for birth control or abortion counseling. They also sometimes threaten physicians and other medical personnel at clinics that perform abortions, and have on occasion threatened the families of these workers (Vetter & Perlstein, 1991, p. 64). The antiabortion group Operation Rescue has repeatedly made news by blocking entrances to health clinics where abortions are performed. Operation Rescue's founder, Randall Terry, and two others leaders, Pat Mahoney and Jim Evans, have all been jailed at various times for this activity (Leavitt, 1991).

Nice (1988), who examined the phenomenon of the bombing of abortion clinics in the United States, notes that these bombings appear to be related to several social factors: Most have occurred in areas with rapidly expanding populations and declining social controls, such as urban areas. The bombings themselves are a form of message, a sign of direct action. Bombing rates have been highest, predictably, in areas where the rate of abortion has been high. One of Nice's most interesting findings is that attacks have tended to occur less frequently in states that have passed strong domestic violence legislation than in those that have not. Finally, Nice reports that the rate of bombings has been low in areas with high populations of Catholics, Baptists, or Mormons. Nice refers to the bombing of abortion clinics as acts of "political violence." The FBI refers to abortion clinic bombings as "criminal felonies" in its annual *Uniform Crime Reports.* It does not report these bombings as acts of terrorism, even though they fit the FBI's own definition (White, 1991, p. 180).

The Jewish Defense League

The Jewish Defense League (JDL) was founded by an attorney, Bert Zweibon, and a rabbi, Meier Kahane, in 1968. The group's purpose is to protect Jews from social and personal mistreatment. Since 1977, there have been more than 43 acts of political terrorism attributed to the JDL; Kahane allegedly advocates the use of violence (Vetter & Perlstein, 1991, p. 64).

Despite their sometimes violent rhetoric, members of the JDL engage in relatively few acts of terrorism (Harris, 1987). Only a small percentage of the group's members have actively pursued terrorist activities; as of 1987, 30 JDL members had been convicted for acts of terrorism in federal courts (Hoffman, 1987, p. 5). They used pipe bombs, firebombs, and smoke bombs against ex-Nazis, Communists, and Arabs living in the United States.

NARCOTERRORISM

Only a decade ago, the international drug trade was not recognized as a source of terrorist activities. This has changed as we have moved closer to the twenty-first century. The United States has a huge appetite for illegal drugs. According to Vetter and Perlstein (1991), 20 million Americans use marijuana regularly, 8-20 million are regular users of cocaine, half a million are heroin addicts, a million use hallucinogens, and almost 6 million abuse prescription drugs (p. 150). Because of this demand, there are tremendous profits to be made by producers and traffickers in illegal drugs.

The Sendero Luminoso and other such groups are actively involved in the business of providing aid to the drug dealers for payoffs in money and influence. The Colombian terrorist group M-19 (which stands for the 19th of April Movement) is another.

This originally was a right-wing youth organization, but it has changed its political philosophy; by the mid-1970s it was engaged in terrorist activities in South America. The M-19 began their terrorist incidents by demanding money from drug dealers for the safe return of the dealers' kidnapped family members. The drug dealers fought back. When the dealers had killed enough M-19 members, a deal was struck between the two previously warring factions. The drug lords paid the members of the M-19 to carry out terrorist acts for them. In acts of gross brutality, the M-19 have killed police, public officials, DEA agents, and other public citizens.

Another similar group is the Colombian Revolutionary Armed Forces (FARC is the acronym of the group's name in Spanish). This group collects protection money from coca growers but grants them early warning of police activities. The FARC controls transportation routes, provides small airfields for planes smuggling drugs out of the country, and participates in sundry other acts that have direct impact on the drug problem in the United States (Vetter & Perlstein, 1991, pp. 151-153).

CONCLUDING REMARKS

The Federal Bureau of Investigation has a legal responsibility to investigate and enforce the laws regarding terrorism within the United States. However, as Stinson (1984) notes, on most occasions the local police are the first level of law enforcement to deal with any problem of domestic terrorism. Granted, most of the time these terrorists fall into Hacker's (1976) category of "criminal." Certainly, general confusion over what constitutes terrorism, inconsistent methods of gathering data, and confusion as to the exact role of the federal government in combating terrorism have combined to produce misunderstanding and perhaps underreporting of terrorist activities. What is known, however, is that over the years a great number of terrorist incidents have occurred within the United States as well as its protectorates.

According to White (1991), most domestic terrorist activity comes out of one of five sources: foreign groups, revolutionary nationalists, the ideological right, the ideological left, and criminals. Examples of foreign terrorists would be such groups as the

Turks and the Armenians in the United States at the turn of the century. White cites the Sandinistas as an example of revolutionary nationalists who have come inside the national boundaries of the United States in drug transactions to fund their war efforts in their own country (p. 167). It is not all that unusual for an outside terrorist group to come across the border of the United States to commit acts of violence. It is also not unusual for groups to attack Americans and their holdings in foreign countries. For example, witness the activities of the Sendero Luminoso (SL), or the Shining Path. Founded by a university professor, Abimael Guzman, this group originally limited its membership to university students and junior faculty members (Vetter & Perlstein, 1991, p. 151). In October 1992, in Peru, Guzman was sentenced to life in prison without parole for his role in the group's terrorist activities. It is currently unclear who has taken over leadership of the SL.

The philosophy of the Shining Path is one of radical communism. The group attempts to spread its message through acts designed to disrupt the functioning of other governments. Estimated membership in the Shining Path is 4,000-5,000. The group avoids direct conflict with the military in South America, and finances many of its activities through ties with South American drug lords, although members are also involved in more mundane criminal activities, such as bank robbery and extortion. The murderous activities of the Shining Path often include gruesome assassinations in which the victims are mutilated and the corpses are left on public display. The display scenario is at least partly related to a religious belief that an unmutilated victim's spirit can reveal its killer. Of course, a more pragmatic reason might be found in the terror effect such displays have on the general public (Vetter & Perlstein, 1991).

Another terrorist organization currently operating is called Macheteros (Machete Wielders). This group is headquartered in Puerto Rico and has been involved in attacks on and murder of U.S. citizens. Macheteros is a tightly organized and violent group fiercely dedicated to the independence of Puerto Rico. The primary target of their acts of terrorism is the United States. Formed in 1978, the group's political objective is to gain independence by waging war against "U.S. colonialist imperialism." Macheteros receives money from sympathizers as well as from

The Shining Path: Selected Incident Chronology

August 1981	Bombed the U.S. embassy, the Bank of America, the Coca-Cola bottler, and a dairy product firm associated with the Carnation Co., all in Lima, Peru.
July 1982	Threw two dynamite bombs at the U.S. embassy in Lima and set off bombs at three private businesses.
May 1982	Blew up 10 electrical power-line towers in a coordinated attack that blacked out Lima, and set off more than 30 bombs, causing $27 million in damage.
October 1983	Bombed the car of a Lima policeman.
August 1984	Burned an evangelical church run by U.S. missionaries in southeastern Peru.
November 1984	Bombed the U.S.-Peruvian Cultural Institute in Lima.
December 1985	Set off a bomb in the Lima airport, killing a child and four other people.
March 1986	Assassinated 3 provincial mayors by shooting them in the head in the town of Chacra Pampas.
June 1986	Bombed a tourist train, killing 8 (including 1 American) and wounding 40 (including 9 Americans).
July 1986	Bombed the Soviet embassy in Lima.
January 1987	Attacked the Indian embassy.
March 1987	Conducted an unsuccessful assassination attempt against the Bank of Tokyo general manager.
April 1987	Attacked the North Korean Mission in Lima, injuring at least 3 people.
November 1987	Attacked the Nissan factory and also the U.S. embassy.
June 1988	Two U.S. Agency for International Development subcontractors were killed while traveling in an area controlled by the SL.

SOURCE: U.S. Department of Justice (1988, pp. 106-111).

robberies and thefts carried out by members. It is uncertain who exactly is the leader of this group; also uncertain is their membership.

The last upsurge of terrorism in the United States took place from the late 1960s to the mid-1970s. At that time most of the activity was inspired by leftist ideology and often involved members of minority ethnic groups. Most groups were spawned along with the civil rights and antiwar movements. Infamous leaders included Eldridge Cleaver, Stokeley Carmichael, H. Rap

Macheteros: Selected Incident Chronology

August 1978	Killed a policeman during a robbery.
December 1979	Killed two sailors in an attack on a U.S. Navy bus.
March 1980	Fired on a bus carrying three ROTC instructors from the University of Puerto Rico.
January 1981	Destroyed eight aircraft and damaged two others in a carefully executed multiple bombing attack on the Air National Guard airfield. Damage was estimated at $40 million.
May 1982	Killed one sailor and wounded three others in an ambush outside a San Juan nightclub.
September 1983	Robbed a Wells Fargo armored truck depot in Hartford, Connecticut. The $7.2 million heist was the second largest in U.S. history.
October 1983	Fired an antitank rocket into the new Federal Building in San Juan to protest U.S. rescue operations in Grenada.
January 1985	Fired an antitank rocket into the Federal Courthouse in San Juan.
November 1985	Shot and wounded a U.S. Army recruiting officer in an ambush while he was on his way to work.
December 1986	Bombed a vehicle at the National Guard Center in Puerto Rico.

SOURCE: U.S. Department of Justice (1988, pp. 92-94).

Brown, and Mark Rudd. Their activities ranged from the burning of draft cards to the killing of police.

Terrorist episodes have continued to the present day, as the above discussion has shown. Fortunately, terrorist threats within the borders of the United States, such as threats to U.S. nuclear facilities, are not currently assessed as high. Terrorists in the United States have generally relied on symbolic bombings and have consistently avoided attacking defended sites. Domestic terrorist groups do not have the funding to launch well-planned attacks on nuclear power plants, for instance (Hoffman, 1987). However, the potential is present and the threat is real.

The U.S. government needs to formulate policies for combating internal acts of terrorism. To combat real and potential terrorist activity effectively, federal authorities need to prepare

Breakdown of Terrorist Incidents in the United States and
Puerto Rico, 1980-1986

State or Territory	Number of Incidents	Percentage
New York	63	33.16
Puerto Rico	57	30.00
Florida	19	10.00
California	15	7.89
District of Columbia	14	7.37
Idaho	5	2.63
Michigan	3	1.58
Illinois	2	1.05
Massachusetts	2	1.05
New Jersey	2	1.05
Texas	2	1.05
Colorado	1	.53
Nevada	1	.53
Oregon	1	.53
Pennsylvania	1	.53
Tennessee	1	.53
Virginia	1	.53
Total	190	100.01

SOURCE: Federal Bureau of Investigation (1986, p. 47).
NOTE: Percentages may not add to 100 because of rounding.

certain strategies. For example, there should be an agency spe-
cifically designated to coordinate international and domestic
terrorism intelligence. Also, government should make clear a
strict policy of no capitulation. It is apparent that direct intervention is the best policy.

Our legal infrastructure is cumbersome, and most state and
local jurisdictions have neither the ability nor the resources to
manage prosecution and imprisonment of terrorists. An example
is the robbery of a Brink's armored truck carried out by BLA
members in 1981. This case required two changes of venue and a
jury selection process that required the screening of 2,600 potential jurors, and it took two to three years to prosecute—all at a total
cost of $5-$7 million. Unless something is done to change the
process in cases of alleged terrorism, our legal structure will
continue to block effective legal action in these cases.

Whether or not the needed legal changes are made, courtroom security requires extensive upgrading for the protection of all involved in terrorism cases. Courtrooms, jails, and prison perimeters, with few exceptions, are easily penetrated by trained professionals and could easily be seized.

Finally, the public must realize that there are a significant number of people in our society who believe that they are not being treated fairly by our legal and social systems. Those in positions of influence and power need to take steps to rectify those situations where perceived injustices are also real.

It may be that acts of terrorism, within the United States and transnationally, do not currently account for an alarming percentage of worldwide violence. Some researchers, however, believe that trends in incidents of terrorism are cyclical (e.g., Harris, 1987). According to this viewpoint, terrorism in the United States is now in the low part of the cycle, and a new generation of terrorists are bound to surface in the near future, with an agenda for political and personal violence. If this is true, we must be prepared for this eventuality.

8

Sex-Related Homicide

Sexually motivated homicide is perhaps the most disturbing of all types of murder. These cases, which often involve sexual mutilation of body parts and/or acts of necrophilia, cannibalism, and vampirism, send the terrifying signal that a sexual psychopath is on the loose. These crimes are all too present in the media. The well-known case of Adam Walsh is an example. This 7-year-old boy, who was abducted from a Hollywood, Florida, shopping center and whose decapitated body was found some time later, was thought to be the victim of a mysoped. Ottis Toole, a sexual sadist and the alleged killing companion of Henry Lucas, at one time confessed to Adam's murder. Currently in prison in Florida, Toole later recanted this confession. The identity of Adam Walsh's killer is still unknown.

Police files are replete with cases involving homicidal offenders who have made a connection between sexual gratification and sexual violence. Most often the violence in these cases is directed against the vulnerable, typically women and children, usually girls. Unless the perpetrator is a homosexual, males are seldom victimized. The 33 victims of John Wayne Gacy are certainly exceptions to this rule, however. Another recent case that is an exception is that of Jeffrey Dahmer in Milwaukee.

WHAT IS SEXUAL HOMICIDE?

For purposes of this discussion, *sexual homicide* is defined as murder that combines fatal violence with a sexual element. One typical element in sexual homicide is fantasy; the perpetrator fantasizes about sexual violence directed toward a helpless victim. This violence usually ends with the killing of the victim, often preceded by various aberrant sexual acts. The following story was related to the first author by Jose M, a sexual sadist. Note the elements of the fantasy, the stalk, and finally the murder.

Five hours. Five long wretched hours had passed. And, still I had not a damn thing to show for the time or the tankful of gas I'd burned up while cruising the highways surrounding my suburban hometown. Off to the west, I could see the sun was already beginning to drop behind the dirty-grey hills which lay several miles away. Soon it would be dark outside, and I'd have but little choice but to call it quits for the day. And the thought of this was so infuriating to me that I smashed my fist against the thinly padded surface of the dashboard of my car as if this eruption of pointed violence could somehow exorcise the raging frustration that was threatening to consume me from within. I was feeling threatened. I was feeling betrayed. I felt as if some cruel and unseen power was toying with me, taunting me, deliberately making my life miserable by denying me what I both craved and deserved.

Yet, for all my resolve to crush and destroy, my shoulders were sagging from the weight of disappointment as I gazed off to the west again. Through the side window of my car, I saw that the sun was now completely below the hilly horizon, and I knew in my gut that this day's hunt was doomed to end in failure. It would only be a matter of minutes before twilight was blanketed by darkness. And, from the countless hunting excursions I'd made before this day, I knew all too well that nightfall's arrival had a maddening way of sweeping my desired prey off the highways, driving them indoors, keeping them impossibly beyond my reach.

Snarling with bitter frustration while switching on my car's headlights, I forced myself to swallow the fact that it was time to call off the hunt. To be sure, I was completely determined to resume my search on the highways tomorrow afternoon, just as soon as I could yank myself away from work. But, tonight, I'd have no use for the jagged-edged knife or the two lengths of rope which were tucked, still hidden, inside my jacket. Nor would I get to enjoy any of the novel punishments that I'd been so eager to try out on some low-life wench. Instead I'd be returning to my home completely alone. Empty-handed. Without the prize I was so desperately craving.

And then it happened. Just when I was counting the day a total loss, all of my nerve-endings bounced alive with excitement at what was being illuminated by the bright glare of my head-lights. I could hardly believe what I was now seeing on the shoulder of the road some fifty yards in front of me. But there, at long last, I'd found what I'd been searching for throughout the entire afternoon: a lone hitchhiker. Yellow-haired and slender. Unmistakably young. Very definitely female. And there she stood, in the traditional beseeching pose, her thumb jutting toward the sky from the end of her outstretched arm.

Instantly, even before I was braking to slow my car's forward momentum, my decision was made: the small, solitary figure on the roadside was MINE. She didn't know it yet, and it would be perhaps awhile before the truth came crashing down upon her. But she now belonged to me. Plain and simple. She was my possession. My personal property. She was ALL MINE—to do with as I damn well pleased.

"Hi! My name is Becky," the girl said brightly, after swinging open the passenger-side door and ducking her head inside. She was a pretty thing, stylishly dressed, probably no more than sixteen or seventeen years old. "Can you give me a lift as far as the Oxmoor Mall?"

I was pleasantly surprised by her stated destination. The mall she'd named was very close to where I lived, which would certainly make things a lot easier on me when it came to luring her to my house. "The Oxmoor Mall? Why, I live only a few blocks from there," I answered truthfully, smiling amiably as I spoke. "So I guess you found yourself the right taxi. Hop on inside, little lady! I'll take you all the way there."

Thanking me several times over as she settled into the seat beside me, the small blonde drew the passenger-door shut, and I slowly pulled my car back onto the highway. I'd given her no cause for any alarm, of course, she was completely oblivious to the fact that my hatred and contempt for her was already a rising storm beneath my outward show of friendliness. For, even as I was smiling at her bubbling words of gratitude, my brain was conducting a fast and furious trial inside the privacy of my skull—and SHE was the one and only defendant. I was judging her. And I was condemning her. I was damning this girl named Becky to a fate that would soon have her wishing she'd never been born.

Jose offered the girl a marijuana cigarette from the glove compartment, knowing there was none there, so that he could then suggest that they go to his house and smoke a joint together, and then he would take her to the mall. At first she refused; but as they drove a few blocks, she finally consented and fell to his ruse.

"Well, Becky, here we are," I announced cheerfully, slowing my car in front of my house and turning onto the driveway. By design, the electrically powered door to my two car garage was already wide open. Also by design, the small control-box for the garage-door closing mechanism was tucked inside my jacket pocket, out of my passenger's view. Allowing my car to glide all the way inside the garage, I braked to a stop, then casually turned off the engine and my headlights.

Instantly, it was difficult to see anything beyond one another's shadowy outline. And, before she could suspect that anything was amiss by this sudden darkness, I was reaching inside my pocket and pressing the button on the control box. Noisily, my automatic garage door started clanking down behind us.

At the sound of the lowering door, the little blonde turned her face toward the rear and then back towards me. As I had no further need to respond to her questions and waste words on a continuing charade, I was silent. Instead, I lashed out my right arm with a hard, back-handed motion, plowing my balled up fist into her stomach. With a loud whooshing sound, the blow knocked all the air out of her of lungs, and she doubled over to get her breath. Then, while she struggled to get her breathing muscles working again, I switched on my car's inside light and knelt on the seat beside her crumpled form, a yard-long piece of rope already in my hand. In my heart, I was the scourge of justice to this worthless tramp, so it bothered me not at all to see her clutching and clawing at her midsection in such obvious pain. Indeed, there was something very reassuring about the sight of her agony. It was a good feeling, a heady feeling, an arousing feeling of complete control. Spurred to action by this frame of mind, I grabbed her by the hair and yanked her up into a sitting position, snapping her head back over the top of my car seat. Quickly, then, my knife was against her throat, and her mouth opening wide in an effort to let out a scream. Inside of a scream, however, only a strangled gasp could escape past her lips.

"OK, pay attention slut. If I hear one more sound out of you, or if you make even one false move, you're gonna be dead real quick. And I mean exactly what I say. Do you get that loud and clear?"

As best she could with my hand still gripping at her hair, my little captive nodded her head up and down just as I expected she would. I pulled out two lengthy pieces of cloth from beneath my seat, using them to cover over her eyes and mouth. When they were tied securely, I let her sit unmolested for a few minutes while I smoked a cigarette. Finally when I finished my cigarette, I flicked off the inside light and pushed open the door of my car. After grabbing her by the arm, then, I pushed the bitch toward me, hauling her across my seat as I stepped onto the floor of my garage. Although she was whimpering and trembling very noticeably, she made no attempt to struggle as I lifted her up and helped her onto her feet.

The killer then was taken by complete surprise when the victim turned toward the front of the garage. She crashed into the garage door panels and started kicking at the door, making loud noises despite the gag in her mouth. Jose ran into her back with his shoulder and sent her sprawling onto a pile of weight-lifting equipment, where a barbell fell on her. The killer lost his balance and also fell on her. Convinced that he had simply knocked the wind out of her, he put Becky over his shoulder and carried her into the house, into his bedroom.

Reaching my bedroom I dumped and locked her inside my closet for the moment, then hurried back to my living room where I peered nervously through the windows. All was quiet in front of my house. I knew in my gut that everything was going to be just fine.

And everything was ready for my little Miss Becky. Indeed, everything had been set-up and laid-out since mid-afternoon when my gut had loudly informed me that this was the day to take up the righteous hunt. Propped against one wall, there was a huge, full-length mirror, where the young wench would watch her own reflection as she stripped away by her own hand all the skin-tight harlot's clothing that she wore and showed off so proudly. And, snaking onto the mattress from the four corners of the bed, there were individual ropes, one for each wrist and ankle, which would stretch her out and hold her down while she received her just desserts. Then, on a low wooden table next to my bed, there rested some of the tools that would assist in her punishment: an assorted collection of heavy leather belts; large pieces of rough grit sandpaper; a plastic box of jagged-tooth metal clips; a bare, scorching-hot light bulb attached to a small, handheld lamp; and, as an added twist, a small container of mace—the very same stuff that females so often loved to spray in the face of their male superiors.

Yes, all of this was ready and waiting for my little captive, and I was seething with anticipation, my temples pounding with excitement, as I pulled back the sliding bolt on the outside of my closet. Slowly, then, I started inching open the door, my fist raised to deliver still another blow to her stomach if she was stupid enough to resist me yet again. And when I saw that her legs were still extended flat upon the closet floor, I threw the door wide open, almost howling out loud from my eagerness to get my hands on the little bitch.

Suddenly, then, I froze where I stood, sensing immediately that something was terribly, terribly wrong. For, instead of reacting to the sound of my presence, the small blonde remained slumped over to one side, looking like a broken doll, her head sagging motionless against her breast. Her skin was an unnatural pasty-white color and several drops of blood stained the snug material on her thigh. She was perfectly still, much too still; her body exhibiting not even a twitch or a flicker of movement. Then, at last, I noticed the swelling and dark discoloration on the front of her neck, and I remembered the sickening crunching sound I had heard in my garage. And, almost at once, I realized that her throat had been crushed on my weight pile and she would never move another muscle on her own again. She was dead.

As the reality of this sank quickly into my brain, my mind just seemed to snap in two, and I exploded into a violent rage. Savagely, I yanked the whore out of my closet by her hair and threw her body onto my bed where I ripped away all her clothes in tattered shreds. Then everything took on the quality of a frenetic but disjointed dream as I was beating her with my fists this moment, whipping her with a leather strap the next, and then stomping her with my feet the minute after that. I was utterly beyond control, snarling like a rabid animal, attacking with all the fury of a madman. And, as I continued to batter the harlot's naked corpse, I became more and more enraged that she would not thrash in agony beneath my frenzied blows, that she would not fill my bedroom with the sound of anguished female screams. Yet I could not stop and face my demons of despair. So I hit and whipped her and kicked her again and again, as if I could somehow smash my way into the world of the dead and make her suffer still.

Once again I had been tricked and fallen victim to a harlot's treachery. So despite all the difficulties of a night-time hunt, I made up my mind to get back onto the highway without delay. The evening was still young, anything was possible.

The minutes passed until they tallied more than an hour. And, once again, I was smiling as I pulled my car onto my driveway for the second time that evening. Pressing gently on the brake pedal, I rolled to a stop inside my open garage, then nonchalantly switched off my ignition and headlights. Instantly, everything was very dark, and I reached inside my jacket to depress the button on a small, rectangular plastic box. Right on cue, my garage door began lowering automatically, and I felt a familiar twist of sudden movement from the passenger seat to my right.

"Hey! What are you doing?" cried a youthful feminine voice. And, just as this shrill voice went silent, my garage door slammed with a boom.

I had not returned empty handed. And the night indeed would be redeemed.

This particular crime reflects several elements of sexual homicide: the killer's fantasy, the hunt, the ruse, the controlled conversation, and, finally, the murder. All indicate the killer's needs as well as his desires. The fantasies in this story are not all that unusual for sexually motivated killing. Consider the case of Daniel Rakowitz, age 28, who was arrested for the murder of Monika Beerle, a former girlfriend. The victim's remains had been reduced so that they fit into a five-gallon bucket, which was found in the baggage claim area of the Port Authority bus terminal in New York City. Police alleged that Rakowitz, a former short-order cook, stabbed Beerle to death when she threatened to leave him, then boiled her body parts to separate flesh from bones and flushed the skin down the toilet. An anthropophagist, he, like Albert Gein, possessed a desire to eat body parts. This consumption of human flesh is accompanied by a sense of erotic excitement and finally sexual gratification. Rakowitz is now serving time in prison.

Myron Lance and Walter Kehlbach, currently in prison in Utah, are two more examples of sexual killers. Their victims were all young males working in gas stations. The victims were taken into secluded areas and killed. According to a psychologist who works at Utah State Prison, Kehlbach spoke of the enjoyment he received when he cut into the flesh of the victims: "It was like cutting foam rubber . . . and the veins sliced like boiled spaghetti" (quoted by A. Carlisle, personal communication, March 28, 1991). Such statements are typical of those made by persons who commit sexual homicide.

ELEMENTS IN SEXUAL HOMICIDES

From a psychological perspective, certain elements are apparent in all sexual life-styles, in those who practice "normal" sexual behaviors as well as in the aberrant sexual personality. In our interviews with sexually motivated serial murderers we have found these elements to be present, and we have also found that in every case the killers attempted to carry their fantasies out on their victims.

Fantasy

Everyone who is sexual has sexual fantasies. This statement can be made without hesitation. Sexual fantasies of many people often center on romance, love, caring, and touching, for example. But with the sexual sadist who is involved in sexual homicide, sexual fantasies contain violent scripts for action. Bondage, mutilation, and other acts of sadism are part of the scenario. The story related by Jose M above contains typical elements of a fantasy script. The manner in which the bed was laid out, with "the four ropes snaking from each corner," the full-length mirror, the can of Mace, even the latch on the *outside* of the closet door—all reflect the killer's fantasy.

More than one killer has mentioned the role of the sexual fantasy in the acts that lead up to their victims' deaths (see, e.g., Holmes, 1990; McGuire & Norton, 1988; Michaud & Aynesworth, 1983; Rule, 1988; Ressler et al., 1988; Stack, 1983). In addition to the elements of fantasy already mentioned, the killer's scenario may include such acts as anthropophagy, necrophilia, and flagellation.

Symbolism

Sex and sexuality are very visible in our society. In the world of advertising, sex is used to sell everything from automobiles to computers and from dishwashing detergent to breakfast cereal. Ads that include sexually attractive models enhance product sales—Madison Avenue has known this for years.

There are two types of symbolisms in sex, fetishes and partialisms. A fetish is an inanimate object to which sex has been visually attached. There are many examples of fetishes: shoes, stockings, underwear, and many others too numerous to list. Certainly, the average person on the street has at least one fetish. One has only to look at pornography to see fetishes popular in our country today. Jerry Brudos, a lust killer currently incarcerated in Oregon, is a shoe fetishist. At times, he forced his wife to wear shoes that he had stolen from other women (Stack, 1983). In interviews, Jose M, whose story appears above, denied particular fondness for any material object. However, he did say he liked "the cheerleader type"; this kind of image served as a visual aphrodisiac for Jose.

A partialism is part of the body to which people have attached sexual significance. Breasts, buttocks, and legs are common partialisms for men in the United States. Buttocks appear to be very popular partialism for women in this country (Holmes, 1991). When an individual needs a fetish or a partialism in order to perform sexually, that person is said to have a paraphilia or perversion.

Sometimes serial killers will favor victims with a particular partialism in common. Once this is determined, such information can be helpful to investigators. However, care must be taken that any information given to the public on this subject be accurate. For example, one author stated that Ted Bundy killed women with long dark hair that was parted in the middle, and this information became part of the profile that police used to link various murder cases in 1974-1978 (Rule, 1983). This was not always the case, however. Among Bundy's victims were Susan Rancourt, who had blonde hair, and Laura Aime, who was a redhead. Kimberly Leach, his last known victim, had short brown hair. But law enforcement leaped upon this simplistic presumption, and women without this partialism felt safe from the "Ted Killer." In effect, this misinformation increased the danger of many women's being victimized by this sexual sadist. Women who did not possess the stated partialism felt quite safe from Bundy and thus were less wary and more vulnerable.

Jose M mentions early in the letter above the partialisms that attract him: female, slender, yellow-haired, unmistakably young. Jose mentioned during an interview that he was not consciously aware of selecting victims who met this description for his sexually sadistic acts. Only after several years of reflection in prison did he become aware of the sexual symbolisms involved in his victim selection.

Ritualism

If something works well in a person's sexual life, he or she will usually continue to practice those rewarding acts. So it is with sexual sadists. These killers will continue to torture and kill until they tire of the "routine." They may then alter slightly the ways in which they select, torture, kill, and dispose of their victims.

Ritualism is present in many human interactions, both sexual and nonsexual. Following a ritual of sorts becomes part of any couple's sexual habits. Interacting in ritualized ways is part of the process of living together.

In sexual sadism, the perpetrator feels the need to repeat his crimes always in the same or similar fashion. This is particularly true of a killer's early crimes. One killer told the first author in an interview that he made his victims repeat aloud some material he had read in a book of pornography that he found in his father's garage when he was 9 years old (this serialist began his lust killings when he was 18). If the victims did not repeat the words as they were instructed, he would quickly kill them. If they cooperated, the kill was prolonged until the complete script (the ritual) was fulfilled.

Compulsion

In interviews with sexual sadists, we have found compulsion to be an integral part of the conversation. This is the sole common element we have found in all the sexual murderers we have studied personally. One killer spoke of the "awful, craving, eating feeling" that became evident when a long time had passed since the last kill. Indeed, Jose M said, "I woke up one morning knowing I was going to kill like I had killed many mornings before." He then remarked, "Killing was the only way for me to placate this feeling." Another sadist called this feeling a "beast," another called it "the entity," and yet another called it "the shadow." Regardless of the name, it is the common element in sexual sadists' personalities.

This feeling of compulsion may overtake the "traditional" manner in which a murderer kills. It may also alter the ideal victim type selected by the sexual killer. One man interviewed by the first author related:

> I drove downtown to pick up a victim. I had not killed in more than a month, and the pit in my stomach announced that the hunt was on. As I drove down Main Street, I saw her. Blond, young, good body. I waited for the light to turn green, but before it did, she got into a car with another man. The knot in my stomach was churning so bad that I announced to myself that the next woman I saw would be mine. The next woman was two 12-year-old girls. I would have not selected them as my victims had not the signal been so strong inside of me.

All sexual persons have some feeling of sexual compulsion, and this feeling certainly has an impact upon sexual behavior. However, when a person can achieve sexual gratification only when the selected partner (victim) does as commanded, compulsion moves into the area of paraphilia.

LUST MURDER

Geberth (1991) makes a distinction between lust murder and sex-related homicide. A former commander of the New York Police Department, now retired, Geberth has traveled across the United States offering seminars on homicide and sex crimes. In his presentations, Geberth defines the lust murder as one typified by a gross sexual assault involving deep personality pathology and including body mutilation and displacement of selected body parts (partialisms) that have sexual significance to the killer.

Although the lust killing is one type of sexual homicide, the lust killer as a sexual psychopath possesses certain distinct characteristics. The psychopath, or sociopath, has received a great deal of attention recently. Conklin (1989) defines a psychopath as "an asocial, aggressive, and highly impulsive person who feels little or no guilt for his antisocial behavior and who is unable to form lasting bonds of affection with other people" (p. 164). Rush (1991) offers a more comprehensive definition: a person who is not insane but who has a severe mental or personality disorder. According to Rush, the psychopath is deficient in the capacity to feel guilt, accept love, and empathize with others (p. 255).

The true sociopath is one who has been thwarted in the development of the personality. This results in a set of behaviors that are aimed at self-fulfillment even at the expense of the needs or safety of another. Psychopaths may come from various backgrounds, but often these individuals will come into contact with the criminal justice system at some time in their lives, because of their reluctance to abide by the rules and regulations of society. It is useful to view psychopathy as a continuum: Few psychopaths operate on a level that is completely unconcerned with the thoughts, feelings, and actions of others; some who are diagnosed as psychopathic show some concern, at least on a superficial level, for the people with whom they come in contact. However, when the psychopathic personality becomes involved in sexual homicide, the crimes are often bizarre in content, with acts of mutilation, necrophilia, and so on.

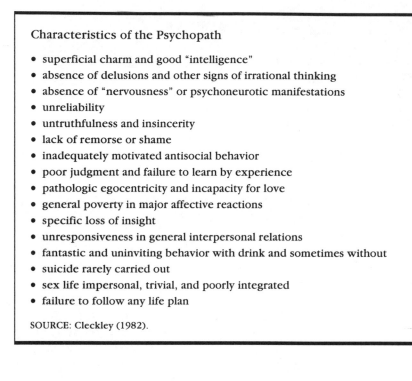

Characteristics of the Psychopath

- superficial charm and good "intelligence"
- absence of delusions and other signs of irrational thinking
- absence of "nervousness" or psychoneurotic manifestations
- unreliability
- untruthfulness and insincerity
- lack of remorse or shame
- inadequately motivated antisocial behavior
- poor judgment and failure to learn by experience
- pathologic egocentricity and incapacity for love
- general poverty in major affective reactions
- specific loss of insight
- unresponsiveness in general interpersonal relations
- fantastic and uninviting behavior with drink and sometimes without
- suicide rarely carried out
- sex life impersonal, trivial, and poorly integrated
- failure to follow any life plan

SOURCE: Cleckley (1982).

The Lust Murderer

The Federal Bureau of Investigation has taken the lead in developing a typology of lust murderers. From an investigation of 36 incarcerated killers (none of whom is identified by name), two polar types of lust murderers were developed: *organized* and *disorganized.* The organized lust murderer tends to be a loner because he wants to be, because he feels others are "unworthy" of this friendship; he is a loner by choice, and the *nonsocial* label signified this. The *asocial* label, on the other hand, signified that the disorganized offender tends to be a loner because others are reluctant to become personally involved with him, because he is somehow strange or bizarre.

The disorganized lust killer is disorganized in his total behavior, in his work and at home; his vehicle, clothing, demeanor, and so on all reflect his disorganized state. The disorganized offender is typically low in intelligence, socially inadequate, living alone, and low in birth order status (that is, is not usually the oldest or the middle child in his family of origin), and usually lives and works near his crime zone. Research suggests that the disorganized offender is often a "non-athletic white male with an introverted personality" (Holmes, 1990, p. 44; Ressler et al., 1988). He has often been physically and/or emotionally abused in childhood.

Disorganized offenders also tend to share several postoffense behaviors. They often return to the scenes of their crimes, and they sometimes even place "in memoriam" personal ads about their victims in local newspapers. These offenders also may change residences (but usually within the same neighborhood) as well as jobs after they kill ("The Men Who Murdered," 1985).

The disorganized offender does not plan his attacks, if for no other reason than lack of ability to do so. He does not usually use restraints on the victim, mostly because the attacks are spontaneous and unplanned, and the victim is simply an object for the use of pointed violence. Often this kind of offender finds victims in the area where both he and the victims live and work, at least in part because this killer feels comfortable only in areas with which he is familiar ("The Men Who Murdered," 1985).

The disorganized offender often disfigures the faces of his victims. He also often mutilates victims' bodies, removing sexual parts and taking these parts with him from the crime scene. Furthermore, his victims' bodies show evidence of a great amount of overkill; that is, they have been subjected to extreme forms of violence.

The crime scene of the disorganized asocial offender is usually quite chaotic, yielding a great deal of physical evidence. This offender does not appear to be nearly as concerned as the organized nonsocial offender about avoiding apprehension.

The organized nonsocial murderer is the theoretical opposite of the disorganized offender. Such exact oppositions seldom exist in reality, but the overall typology is an important starting point for an examination not only of the offenders themselves but also of the crime scenes they leave behind.

The organized offender is neat and organized in everything he or she does. This offender's workplace, home, car, and personal appearance all reflect the need for order, cleanliness, and neatness. The organized offender may be said to be anal

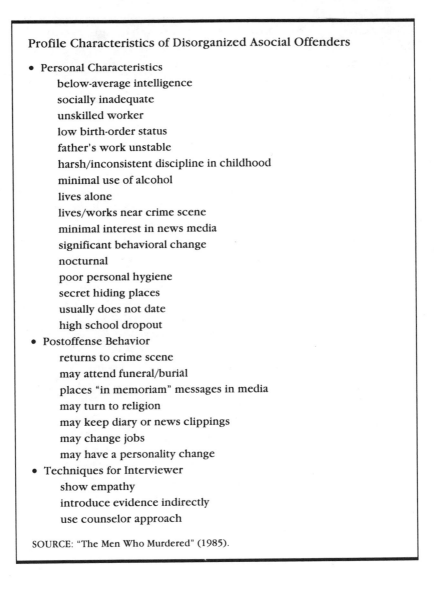

Profile Characteristics of Disorganized Asocial Offenders

- Personal Characteristics
    below-average intelligence
    socially inadequate
    unskilled worker
    low birth-order status
    father's work unstable
    harsh/inconsistent discipline in childhood
    minimal use of alcohol
    lives alone
    lives/works near crime scene
    minimal interest in news media
    significant behavioral change
    nocturnal
    poor personal hygiene
    secret hiding places
    usually does not date
    high school dropout
- Postoffense Behavior
    returns to crime scene
    may attend funeral/burial
    places "in memoriam" messages in media
    may turn to religion
    may keep diary or news clippings
    may change jobs
    may have a personality change
- Techniques for Interviewer
    show empathy
    introduce evidence indirectly
    use counselor approach

SOURCE: "The Men Who Murdered" (1985).

retentive in personality type; there is a place for everything and everything must be in its place. This offender is nonsocial because he chooses to be so. In everyday life, this offender believes that no one is good enough for him to risk friendship with.

Crime Scene Traits of the Disorganized Lust Killer

- spontaneous offense
- victim/location known
- depersonalizes victim
- minimal conversation
- crime scene is random and sloppy
- sudden violence to the victim
- minimal use of restraints
- sexual acts after death
- body left in view
- evidence/weapon often present
- body left at death scene

SOURCE: "The Men Who Murdered" (1985).

The FBI suggests that there may be precipitating factors in lust murders of the organized type ("The Men Who Murdered," 1985). Stress may trigger a killing, but because of the perpetrator's organized personality, he can delay the kill itself. For example, one lust killer currently in prison in a western state told the first author in an interview that he killed one young woman because she dared to look at another man while she was out on a date with him. This was enough for him to go into an emotional tirade that resulted in her death. Her murder was accompanied by sadistic sexual torture and dismemberment. Although at first glance this may seem like the work of a disorganized killer, further examination shows that although the external stressor was the motivation for the murder, the killer still behaved in an organized manner. He took the victim to his "comfort zone," involved himself in a "process" kill, and then disposed of the body.

Other personal characteristics of the organized offender include high intelligence, social adeptness, and relative ease in adjusting to new situations. Many organized offenders appear to have normal sex lives; often they have spouses or live-in partners. These offenders tend to be both occupationally and spatially mobile, and they usually have no particular need to stay in familiar areas ("The Men Who Murdered," 1985).

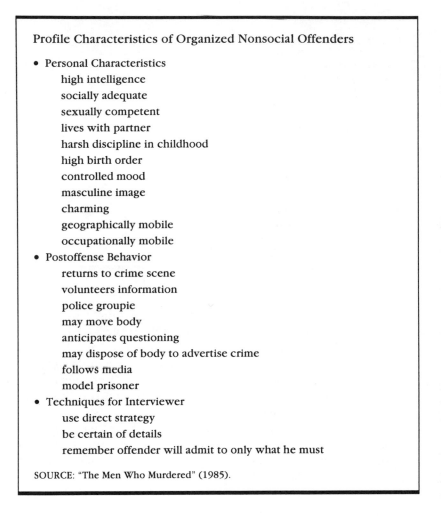

Profile Characteristics of Organized Nonsocial Offenders

- Personal Characteristics
    high intelligence
    socially adequate
    sexually competent
    lives with partner
    harsh discipline in childhood
    high birth order
    controlled mood
    masculine image
    charming
    geographically mobile
    occupationally mobile
- Postoffense Behavior
    returns to crime scene
    volunteers information
    police groupie
    may move body
    anticipates questioning
    may dispose of body to advertise crime
    follows media
    model prisoner
- Techniques for Interviewer
    use direct strategy
    be certain of details
    remember offender will admit to only what he must

SOURCE: "The Men Who Murdered" (1985).

The organized offender who is a true psychopath has little trouble making friends, but he keeps all friendships on a superficial level. Ted Bundy's ability to charm is an excellent example. In interviews, the first author found that Bundy was so capable of putting a person at ease that after five minutes it seemed that he had known this serial killer for years. This is one reason these murderers are so effective.

Crime Scene Traits of the Organized Lust Killer

- planned offense
- targeted stranger
- personalizes victim
- controlled conversation
- controlled crime scene
- submissive victim
- aggressive acts
- restraints used
- body moved
- weapon taken
- little evidence

SOURCE: "The Men Who Murdered" (1985).

Unlike the disorganized offender, the organized lust killer uses restraints on his victims. The kill is process focused (Holmes, 1989; see also Chapter 6 of this volume).

The organized offender, according to the research of the FBI, not only commits the crime in a fashion much different from that of the disorganized offender, he behaves differently after the crime is committed. For example, the organized killer will often move the body from the kill site to a disposal site. There may be committed acts of sexual mutilation and dismemberment as well as a variety of other sexual aberrations.

The following list notes some of the paraphilias involved in lust murder (for more on this subject, see Geberth, 1991, p. 71; Holmes, 1991):

- *fetishism:* use of nonliving objects for sexual arousal (female undergarments, panties, shoes, and so on)
- *transvestism:* cross-dressing by heterosexual male for sexual excitement (ranges from solitary wearing of female clothes to extensive involvement in a transvestite subculture)
- *zoophilia:* use of animals for sexual arousal (includes intercourse with animals as well as training animals to lick or rub a human partner)

- *pedophilia:* engaging in sexual activity with prepubertal children
- *exhibitionism:* exposing the genitals to an unsuspecting stranger for the purpose of obtaining sexual excitement
- *voyeurism:* repetitive looking at unsuspecting people who are naked, in the act of disrobing, or engaging in sexual activity
- *sexual masochism:* getting pleasure from being humiliated, bound, beaten, or otherwise made to suffer for sexual arousal (considered a chronic disorder)
- *sexual sadism:* infliction of physical or psychological pain on another person in order to achieve sexual excitement (considered a chronic and progressive disorder)
- *atypical paraphilias:* a residual category listed in the American Psychiatric Association's (1987) *Diagnostic and Statistical Manual of Mental Disorders*; includes individuals with paraphilias that cannot be classified in any of the other categories (including coprophilia, sexual attraction to feces; frotteurism, sexual attraction to rubbing against the genitalia or body of another; klismaphilia, sexual attraction to giving or receiving enemas; mysophilia, sexual attraction to filth; necrophilia, sexual attraction to dead bodies; telephone scatologia, sexual attraction to making obscene telephone calls; lewdness; and urophilia, sexual attraction to urine)

Sex-related homicide can involve an interesting blend of various levels of sex behaviors. The lust killer may be involved in more than simply aberrant sexual practices; he may have an added propensity for sadism and violence, and for such acts as anthropophagy, necrophilia, erotic asphyxiation, and picquerism. In addition, elements of pyromania or infibulation are sometimes present. Crimes of sexual violence are often connected with many of these paraphilias.

Anthropophagy

Anthropophagists receive sexual gratification from the eating of the flesh (more commonly called cannibalism) or drinking of the blood (more commonly called vampirism) of a victim (Holmes, 1991, p. 116). There are several examples of cannibals in the recent criminal justice history. Ted Bundy, for example, bit off a nipple of one of his victims and ingested it (Michaud & Aynesworth, 1983).

Albert Fish cooked body parts of several of his victims (Schechter, 1990). Ed Gein was also an anthropophagist (Gollmar, 1982). Ressler et al. (1988) believe that murderers involved in cannibalism may be more likely to be disorganized offenders than organized offenders. (Ted Bundy, of course, was an organized personality type. He, like perhaps some others, is an exception to the rule, as Ressler et al. note.) They discuss one case in which the victim had knife wounds to the breasts, intestines, and internal reproductive organs, and note that "a yogurt cup was found, and indications were that the murderer used the cup to collect blood from the victim, which he then drank" (p. 132). In a recent case in a southern state, an aeronautical engineer was arrested after he had killed eight women. He drank their blood, which he stored in a refrigerator until his passion impelled him to drink.

It is unclear what leads individuals to find sexual gratification in the eating of flesh or the drinking of blood. What is clear is that those who have begun these practices will tend to continue them.

Necrophilia

Perhaps one of the most bizarre of sexual practices is that of necrophilia, sex with the dead. Necrophilia is a predominantly male paraphilia, however, a few female necrophiliacs have been noted in the literature (see, e.g., A. Ellis, 1986; Freire, 1981). Douglas Clark, the Hollywood Strip Killer, allegedly decapitated his female victims and used the heads in sexual acts (Farr, 1992).

There are numerous other examples of necrophiliacs who have been arrested for their acts and sent to prison. Necrophilia is not as rare in sex-related crimes as was once thought (Bartholomew, Milte, & Galbally, 1978; Brill, 1941; Burg, 1982). Again, Ted Bundy provides an example. He kept one victim, a young woman from Utah, for nine days after he killed her. He stated in an interview with the first author that he kept her under his bed, in his closet, and on his bed. After all, he said, there was no rush to remove the body because he knew no one would be coming to his apartment. He sexually assaulted her for eight days after he had killed her. Jerry Brudos, a serial killer, admitted to having sexually assaulted two of his four known victims after they were dead (Rule, 1988).

There are considered to be three levels of necrophilia. The first level involves only fantasy. At this level sexual pleasure is gained from pretending that one's sexual partner is dead at the time of intercourse; there is no wish actually to have a sexual encounter with a dead body. There is a clear understanding that the partner is "only playing." This type of fantasy is fairly common among men who frequent prostitutes. One prostitute told the first author about two of her customers who pay her to pretend to be dead, one a university dean and the other an attorney. One of the men wanted only to look at her as she lay completely still on the bed (Holmes, 1991, p. 59).

A second type of necrophiliac is one who has a sexual relationship with someone who is already dead. This type of paraphiliac will often deliberately place himself in work situations that allow access to dead bodies: as a funeral home or morgue worker, coroner or deputy coroner, and so on. According to Ressler et al. (1988), this type of person usually is classifiable as a disorganized offender.

The third type of necrophiliac, and clearly the most dangerous, is the necrosadistic offender. This person kills so that he can have sex with a corpse. As Money (1984) notes, the act of sadistic necrophilia must be viewed as the ultimate and most extreme form of erotic eligibility distancing. Rosman and Resnick (1989) note that only a few necrophiles are of the necrosadistic variety; most will simply take advantage of situations where they have ready access to dead bodies.

No one knows the exact cause of necrophilia. By examining the fantasies, however, Calef and Weinshel (1972) and Faguet (1980) offer a psychodynamic explanation: The offender wants to return to the maternal body. Others believe that necrophiliacs are feebleminded (H. Ellis, 1946) or possess gross personality defects (Katchadourian & Lunde, 1975). What is certain is that the victim is dead and can offer no resistance to the sexual advances of the perpetrator (Holmes, 1991; Weeks, 1986).

Pyromania

Pyromania is eroticized fire setting. It is a pathological condition that is characterized by a sense of psychological compulsivity and one that the offender has a great deal of difficulty in containing. Of course, not all cases of fire setting involve pyromaniacs. Some fires are set for insurance purposes, some for business recovery purposes, and others as a means of personal revenge. It is eroticized fire setting that is the focus of this section. Masters and Robertson (1990), for example, state that they have found that as many as 40% of all set fires are caused by pyromaniacs. This estimate may be too high; unfortunately, there is no way we can currently validate this statistic.

Pyromaniacs set fires from a feeling of sexual compulsion. There is an erotic component to the fire-setting act itself, and the fire setter becomes sexually aroused even to the point of involuntary orgasm while watching a fire he has set and all of the commotion that surrounds the fire fighters and the flames.

It is unknown what launches a person into compulsive and erotic fire setting. Bourget and Bradford (1987) believe that often some type of situational cause initiates the action. They recount the story of a young adult arrested for a series of fire settings. When his social case history was taken, the adult was found to have been greatly interested in fires as a child; however, he did not start his first fire until he was an adult. He had been rejected by women he attempted to meet at a local bar, and in a fit of rage he set fire to the bar. This was his first in a series of fires. He connected a sexual component with his feeling of a need to set fires. When he believed he was rejected by a young woman, he would set a fire. He would fantasize about the women in the crowd who were watching the fire and become sexually aroused. Leaving the scene, he would masturbate. Later, a sense of power became a part of the eroticized fire-setting scenario. Money (1984) reports a similar case in his studies of pyromaniacs.

Pyromania is a very dangerous sex crime that unfortunately often results in the deaths of innocent persons. Great care must be taken in the detection and treatment of those involved in this crime. Unfortunately, too little is known about the etiology and the treatment perspectives of this form of sex offender; it is clear that more research needs to be done.

CONCLUSION

This chapter has focused on very dangerous sex crimes that too often result in death. Victims of these crimes are carefully selected in some instances; in others they just happen to be in the wrong place at the wrong time. We have addressed the victim selection process, the role of fantasy, and the carrying out of the homicidal act. In all instances mentioned in this chapter, sex plays an integral role in the commission of the crimes discussed. The typology of the lust killer, organized and disorganized, presents an interesting model for investigation.

It is apparent that for some offenders sex plays an important role in the commission of homicide. In Chapter 6, we noted that some serial killers are also sexual murderers, but that there are other types of serial killers as well. In this chapter we have focused exclusively on sex-related homicide. All of these killers have made the connection between fatal violence and personal gratification, a connection that is in many cases impossible to disrupt.

9

Children Who Kill

Few things are more unsettling than stories of young children who kill. Fortunately, few children resort to fatal violence as a solution to perceived interpersonal problems. Of course, even these few are too many.

While the first author was lecturing at a school for homicide detectives in Boulder, Colorado, a murder case made the front page in that city. The newspaper account described a courtroom scene of an 11-year-old boy standing patiently in front of the judge, with his hands in his pockets and his hair neatly brushed to one side. The headline stated that the boy had killed his father with a .22 hunting rifle while the man slept. The motive—the child was angry because his father made him go to school. Murders such as this one are appalling, and they appear to be increasing. Such cases remind us all too graphically that children can murder, and they are doing it with more regularity than ever before.

Peter Kurten, a serial killer from Europe, killed two children before he was 9 years old. He was playing on a raft on the Rhine River with two playmates. He pushed one boy into the river. The child could not swim and drowned. The other boy dove into the water to save him. Kurten managed to push him under the raft; he also died. Since there was no one to see the act, no one suspected young Kurten (Holmes, 1983).

Ted Bundy killed his first victim when he was 15 (Holmes & De Burger, 1988). Ann Marie Burr was an 8-year-old girl who lived close to Bundy's uncle in Tacoma, Washington. Bundy took her to a small apple orchard, strangled her, and bludgeoned her to death. He then dumped her body in a ditch that was next to her home because the public works department was constructing new sewers and sidewalks in the neighborhood (Ted Bundy, personal communication, November 17, 1987). Mrs. Burr told the first author in a 1987 telephone interview that she remembered that the original suspect was a 16-year-old boy who also lived in the neighborhood. While the police were questioning her on her front porch, she looked out at the crowd that had gathered in the front yard. Bundy was there, kicking dirt into the ditch with his foot. Ann's body was never found.

There are other cases of children who kill. Some of these killings are connected with other crimes; some result from poor personal relationships. Still others may be Satanic or ritualistic crimes. Take, for example, the case of Sean Sellers. Believing himself to be the high priest of his grotto, Sean took the lives of his stepfather and his mother. He believed Satan wanted him to kill his first-born (Sean was unmarried with no children) or his most beloved, and his mother was his most beloved (Wedge, 1988). His commandment to kill rested outside his psyche. The motivation to kill came from his belief in Satanism and his interpretation that *The Satanic Bible* (LaVey, 1969) demanded that he kill for Satan.

Only recently in Pasadena, California, two teenage boys were found guilty in the shotgun slayings of three teenage girls. The victims, Katherine Macaulay, 18, Danae Palermo, 17, and Heather Goodwin, 18, were at a social gathering with the boys when an argument developed. The nature of the argument was so insignificant that it has now been forgotten. The killers, 16 and 17, were convicted in August 1992.

These are not isolated cases. It is entirely possible the number of victims will increase and the stories will become commonplace.

Ample research has investigated the relationships between murderers and their victims. For example, both racial and age differentials have been found. Homicide is the leading cause of death in young black males, and the overwhelming majority of these victims are murdered by other black males (Poinsett, 1987,

p. 90). This may be explained in part by the conditions in many U.S. inner cities. There are many pressures that young males are exposed to in the course of living in poverty. Anomie, lack of opportunities, social isolation, drug use, and racism all contribute to the social problem of murder. The violence that can become a part of everyday relationships under such conditions helps to account for the victimization of young black males by other young black males.

MICHAEL: A CASE STUDY

In a western state, a young man sits in prison for the murder of a 75-year-old woman. This is not the first person he killed; it is his eighth known victim. He has by his admission killed more than 15 persons, and his rapes number more than 50. In an interview the first author conducted with him while both were waiting to appear on a national television talk show, Michael answered some questions regarding his past and drew some interesting conclusions.

This 18-year-old has a criminal history that began at age 8. He had been in various foster homes as well as juvenile institutions as many as 10 times. While in the various institutions, he had successfully escaped more than 35 times. The charges for which he was incarcerated included two thefts in the second degree, two criminal trespass, one arson in the third degree, four burglaries in the first degree, one burglary in the second degree, one sodomy in the first degree, one rape in the second degree, two assaults in the first degree, one assault in the fourth degree, one minor possession of alcohol, one robbery in the first degree, two robberies in the third degree, six charges of driving under the influence of alcohol, and one charge of falsifying information to a police officer.

Michael has freely admitted the stabbing death of a young man in a juvenile institution, and has appeared before judges in the juvenile system 44 times for various offenses. During the interview, Michael was very careful in his confession, never admitting information that could later be used against him in a court of law.

RMH: Michael, you were 16 years old when the stabbing death occurred. Tell me how it felt to kill somebody.

Michael: At the time I was scared, and it wasn't that hard to do once I had my mind set on what I was going to do. A lot of curiosity, I didn't know what I was going to do because I had never done it [committed a murder] before. I didn't know what was going to happen. After I walked up and stabbed him the first time, then I was really scared. It was easier to stab him the second time.

RMH: How many times did you stab him?

Michael: Thirty-six times.

RMH: Why was it necessary to stab him so many times?

Michael: I don't know.

RMH: How did it feel when you were doing it?

Michael: I felt scared, like it was in slow motion. Everything was going in slow motion. He didn't scream or anything like that. He just said, "Huh" or something like that. After I stabbed him, he fell face down on the pavement, that's when I took the wallet out of his pocket. I started to run, and then I started laughing.

RMH: You just stabbed someone and you started laughing?

Michael: It felt good. I thought it was funny at the time. I had just killed someone, and it was better than I thought it would be. It was fun.

RMH: How did you choose him? To rob him and kill him.

Michael: I wanted to go to the mall and rob someone. This didn't work out. I came back toward home and decided that I wasn't coming home empty-handed and broke. I was mad. As I got close to home I decided that the next person I saw I was going to rob. That guy was just the next person I saw.

RMH: When did you decide to kill him?

Michael:	When it [the robbery] got started, he put his hands up. I told him to put his hands down. I didn't want a car to come by and see him with his hands up. I held him up with a knife. He put his hands up and I told him to put his hands down. He got scared and put his hands up again. I told him to put them down. He put them up for the third and last time. When he put them down he put them behind his back. And I stabbed him.
RMH:	So he was not offering any resistance?
Michael:	No. But he just wasn't doing what I had said. He kept putting his hands up. He just kept putting them up. I think he was scared.
RMH:	Is the feeling of killing someone different from the feeling of raping somebody?
Michael:	Yes . . . no. Not really. Because killing someone happens too fast. You know, that rush of adrenaline? In a rape you can make the rape last as long as you want it to. The power feeling is different also. It's much greater with a kill.
RMH:	You have been out of custody for almost six months. Why have you not killed?
Michael:	Because I feel guilty for the next person I am gonna kill. I don't feel bad at all for the last person I killed. Because he's dead, and there's nothing you can do to bring him back. I have never felt bad about any of the crimes I've done. Only once, I take that back. I felt bad about the time I stole something from my mom. I feel bad about that. When I hurt my family, that's the only time I feel bad.
RMH:	What is the most violent crime you ever committed?
Michael:	The robberies and the rapes.
RMH:	This was more violent than the murders? Why?
Michael:	Because the persons lived through it, and they have to live with it for the rest of their lives. For example,

I went to a house of two faggots. I walked in the
house to rob 'em. I knew who and what they were
when I walked in the house. They started giving me
some gin. I was sitting there talking with them and
then told them I was gonna rob them. I pulled a
pistol on them and made them take their clothes
off. They didn't want to but I was acting crazy and
they did what I told 'em to do. I sat back down on
the couch and smashed a little red ashtray on the
coffee table. I told them both to get down on the
floor, tied both of their hands naked with a radio
extension cord and their feet with a flannel shirt.
Then I called them a bunch of names, poured gin
on them, spit on them, stuff like that. Then the
landlady walked in. I pulled her in the room. One
of the homosexuals was her son and the other was
his boyfriend. She kept saying, "You don't want to
do this, You don't want to do this." I told her to
shut up. When she saw them tied up on the floor,
she put her hands up to her mouth and I told her to
get undressed, and she said no. I tore the blouse off
of her, and when I pulled it, the buttons started
busting off. I cocked the gun, and then she started
taking off her clothes and stuff. And the one guy
tried to close his eyes, her son kept trying to close
his eyes and stuff like that. I put my knife under his
chin and told him to watch. And then I proceeded
to rape his mother while she was laying on the floor
next to him. Then I put his mother in the shower
and went back upstairs. I shot a hole in the floor
and missed him [laughing], and then I left. When it
came time for the case to come to court, the mother
and son were told that I would be tried as a juvenile
and would be out when I was 18. They decided not
to press charges and moved out of state. So the case
was thrown out cause they wouldn't testify.

RMH: Do you feel any remorse about this?

Michael: No. But there is always a justification. For the murder,
            there was money. The homosexuals deserved what

happened. But sometimes I did something that there was no justification. Sometimes during the robberies I was just greedy. I just wanted to do it. In a rape, the justification, I was sexually abused when I was 14. This was my justification, my best one.

RMH: Who sexually abused you?

Michael: My uncle abused me sexually when I was 14. I decided to press charges but the attorney for the court wouldn't do anything about it because of who I was. The whole thing stopped. I was wasted. I have the right to be mad, and I want to kill him but if I did I would go to prison. I'm not a juvenile anymore.

Michael was indeed physically and sexually abused. He believes that children who kill are different from adults who kill. He said that "the juvenile who kills usually does not kill the person he is mad at, they kill somebody else that reminds them of who they are mad at." Michael believes that the role of fantasy plays a great part in homicides perpetrated by children: "Kids have a bigger imagination about the ways things should be than adults do." When Michael was quite young, his father was sent to prison. His parents divorced and his mother remarried. There was a great deal of physical abuse in the family. His mother was a victim of spouse abuse by both Michael's father and his stepfather. As a 7-year-old, Michael stole a quarter-pound packet of marijuana. His stepfather accused him of stealing the marijuana and cut two of Michael's fingers off.

Michael believes that almost every child he has known in his years in institutions who has been incarcerated for homicide has been physically and sexually abused. He believes "99%" have been abused in both fashions. He said that he could recall only 1 young man out of more than 30 in his last three years in a juvenile institution who had not been abused. Michael's opinions are supported by research that has been conducted with children who kill. Ewing (1990) notes that "probably the single most consistent finding in the research on juvenile homicide to date is that children and adolescents who kill, especially those who kill family members, have generally witnessed and/or been directly victimized by domestic violence" (p. 22). Child sexual abuse has also been cited as a catalyst for homicidal behavior later in life (Lewis & Grant, 1983; Sendi & Blomgren, 1975). In addition, parental discord in the home apparently has some impact on the mind-set of the youth who kills; physical, sexual, and verbal abuse of the children and/or the mother can play a role (Goetting, 1993; Heide, 1993; Toupinm, 1993).

Michael is currently in prison for the rape and murder of a young woman he stalked for more than six months. As noted above, he experienced both sexual and physical abuse in his family, and he watched his mother being abused not only by his father but by his stepfather as well. He was a behavioral problem in school and truancy was a normal behavior for him. He feels no remorse for what he has done and looks forward to the next time he can victimize someone. Luckily, he will be in prison for at least the next 10 years.

STATISTICS ON CHILD HOMICIDE

Children who kill make up a small percentage of all homicides, and the number of children incarcerated for homicide in state-operated correctional institutions is very small. According to the *Sourcebook of Criminal Justice Statistics,* as of 1989 only 1.8% of all incarcerated youth (those under the age of 18) were incarcerated for murder or nonnegligent manslaughter (U.S. Department of Justice, BJS, 1991b, p. 556). Compare this with the 45.6% of incarcerated youth who were in custody for property offenses (in particular for burglary, 23.8%).

Some external forces may partially account for the low proportion of youth in correctional institutions for homicide. First, many children who kill are committed to psychiatric settings, not correctional facilities. Second, some children accused of murder, especially those who have extensive juvenile records, may be referred to the adult courts for trial and adjudication.

The *Sourcebook* also indicates that 2.0% of all children who were incarcerated for homicide as of 1989 had previously murdered, and almost one-third had been involved in violent personal offenses prior to the homicidal offense for which they were then incarcerated (U.S. Department of Justice, BJS, 1991b,

TABLE 9.1
Arrests of Juveniles for Murder and Nonnegligent Homicides, 1987-1990

Year	Total Homicides	Youth Arrested Under Age 15		Youth Arrested Ages 15-17		Total Juvenile Homicides
		No.	%	No.	%	
1987	16,714	203	1.2	1,389	8.3	1,592
1988	16,326	201	1.2	1,564	9.6	1,765
1989	17,975	290	1.6	1,918	10.7	2,208
1990	18,298	283	1.5	2,272	12.4	2,555

SOURCE: U.S. Department of Justice, BJS (1991b).

p. 567). In contrast, almost 70% of the juveniles who were incarcerated for property crimes as of 1989 admitted to having committed previous crimes.

Children under the age of 15 account for only 1% of homicide arrestees (U.S. Department of Justice, BJS, 1991b). Perhaps a better index of the social problem of children who kill can be gained from the arrests records accumulated by federal registries. Table 9.1 shows homicide arrest data for juveniles from 1987 through 1990. It is apparent from the table that there has been a general increase in the number of children who have been arrested for murder and nonnegligent homicide, especially in the age range of 15-18.

In 1984, juveniles accounted for 7.34% of all persons arrested for murder and nonnegligent homicide. This proportion increased to 11.6% by 1990 (U.S. Department of Justice, BJS, 1991b, pp. 452-453). In sum, it appears that not only are the raw numbers increasing as far as juveniles are concerned, but the percentage of juvenile offenders compared with adult offenders is increasing also.

The propensity for murder appears to increase with the increasing age of the juvenile. For example, as Table 9.2 shows, in 1990, less than 1% of all children who killed were under age 10. More than one in every four cases of juvenile homicide in that year was committed by a 16-year-old, and almost 50% of all homicides carried out by juveniles were committed by 17-year-olds—individuals who are almost adults, according to most legal standards.

TABLE 9.2
Juveniles Arrested in the United States for Murder and Nonnegligent
Homicide, by Age, 1990

Age	Number	Percentage
Under 10	5	.002
10-12	21	.008
13-14	257	10.06
15	445	17.42
16	771	30.08
17	1,056	41.33

SOURCE: U.S. Department of Justice, BJS (1991b, pp. 440-441).

MURDER WITHIN THE FAMILY

A minority of children who commit homicide kill their parents or other family members. Rowley, Ewing, and Singer (1987) found in their sample of 787 juvenile homicide cases that less than 20% were arrested for the murder of a parent or other member of the family (p. 7). The children involved in fatal violence were more apt to kill acquaintances (49.17%) or strangers (33.17%). When theft was a motivating factor in the murder, seldom was a family member involved. When a family member was murdered, in more than four out of five cases only one perpetrator was involved.

Rowley et al. also found the sex of the perpetrator to play an important role in the selection of the victim. For example, when a female juvenile killed, in 93% of the cases the victim was either a family member (44%) or an acquaintance (49%). When male juveniles killed, a family member was the victim less than 14% of the time.

The apparent differences in rates of murder of family members according to the sex of the killer may possibly be accounted for by societal norms. Girls may tend to feel trapped when they find themselves in situations of abuse or neglect, and may see violence as the only way out. In our culture, it is easier and more acceptable for boys to escape from undesirable situations at home. Male juveniles also are more involved than are female juveniles in a variety of crimes that are sometimes of a violent nature, such as assault and robbery. Stranger-to-stranger crimes, including murder, may be more "available" to boys than to girls, and this may help account for the greater percentages of these types of crimes among boys.

YOUTH HOMICIDE AND OTHER CRIME

Many studies have attempted to examine the phenomenon of children who kill (see, e.g., Hamparian, Davis, Jacobson, & McGraw, 1985; Hamparian, Schuster, Dinitz, & Conrad, 1978; Lewis, Shanok, Grant, & Ritvo, 1983; Lewis et al., 1985), but we still know very little about this subject. One study that has added significantly to the knowledge base on this topic was conducted by Goetting (1989), who examined 55 homicidal juvenile offenders incarcerated in Detroit over the years 1977-1984. Goetting found that an overwhelming number of the offenders in her sample were black. This should not be too startling, as the black population of Detroit is quite high, 63% at the time of the study. However, black youth accounted for 81.9% of homicide arrests. The young blacks who murdered were unlike their older counterparts; they were more apt to kill outside their own race and to kill someone slightly older.

For most of Goetting's subjects the homicidal act was the first contact with the criminal justice system. Some 40% had had at least one other contact with the system, and 9% of the offenders were considered to have significant problems in school that resulted in their receiving personal counseling in school as discipline problems.

The families of the youthful killers were often dysfunctional. This dysfunction was measured by many elements, including parents' marital status. Most of the mothers had no mates at the time of the incidents. In many of the remaining families the fathers had remarried.

Many of the families had moved to Detroit from southern states: 70% of the fathers and 48% of the mothers had migrated from the South.[1] Coupled with this migratory experience was overrepresentation in a deprived social class. Unemployment, receiving welfare, and living in urban areas all appeared to play some part in murder. The killers were most often legitimately born; their parents came from large families. In addition, they had few social opportunities to explore and expand their social and cultural life.

Concerning the victims, a general profile emerged that has significance for victimology. Victims were most likely to be other black males (although the likelihood was greater for murders committed by older perpetrators), slightly older than the youths, and killed with a firearm in a home. Sometimes the home was the residence of the killer (16.7%), sometimes the home of both the victim and the killer (18.8%), and sometimes another residence (14.6%). The act itself often was often carried out in the heat of passion, during a confrontation between the killer and the victim. Most of the murders occurred in residences on Tuesdays, Thursdays, or Fridays, between 2:00 p.m. and 1:59 a.m. Most of the deaths were caused by gunshots.

Goetting's study clearly offers a significant amount of data that can be useful for understanding youth who kill. Such scholarly work is to be admired.

THE ETIOLOGY OF
THE JUVENILE HOMICIDAL OFFENDER

There is a vast difference between characteristics and causes. We may be able to say that juvenile homicide is most likely to occur on certain days of the week or with particular weapons, but this does not explain why a particular juvenile resorts to fatal violence as a solution to a perceived need. Since the mid-1950s, various studies have attempted to explain the basic etiology of the juvenile killer. For example, some researchers have taken a biological or medical approach, examining juveniles who have experienced serious physical problems, such as epilepsy, EEG abnormalities, and limbic disorders, but they have all been relatively unsuccessful in explaining homicidal behavior (e.g., Lewis & Shanok, 1977; Pontius, 1982; Satterfield, Hoppe, & Schell, 1982). Other studies have examined the aspect of psychological control over homicidal behavior. The controls investigated appear to be grossly inadequate to circumvent the behaviors that result in the exercise of fatal violence (Brickman, McManus, Grapentine, & Alessi, 1984; Broder, Dunivant, & Smith, 1981; Lewis et al., 1988).

Experts in the field have often relied on diagnoses of mental illness to account for the perpetration of homicide by adolescents. For example, McKnight, Mohr, and Quinsey (1966) found that the majority of the juvenile killers they studied received psychiatric diagnoses that included epilepsy, manic depression, schizophrenia, and psychopathic personality. Some 55% were judged unfit to stand trial, and 27% were found not guilty by reason of insanity. It must be remembered, however, that the juveniles in this study had all been incarcerated in a prison hospital. Other researchers have found similar results. In a study by Lowenstein (1989) of children who murder, psychological influences were found, including low IQ, low levels of tolerance for frustration, history of mental illness, low self-esteem, and severe problems in interpersonal relationships. The influence of mental illness has also been found in other studies (e.g., Reinhardt, 1973; Sendi & Blomgren, 1975). On the other hand, Wolfgang and Ferracuti (1967) found in their classic study that only 3% of their sample were insane. Wong and Singer (1973) also found a low proportion of mental illness among their sample of killers; only 7% were considered to be mentally ill. Thus it is apparent that many studies do not support psychological/psychiatric explanations for the etiology of adolescent homicide.

Studies considering the roles of family background, family violence, gang participation, parental mental illness, and social class in adolescent homicide (e.g., Deykin, Levy, & Wells, 1987; Duncan & Duncan, 1971; Statten, Menninger, & Rosen, 1960; Sendi & Blomgren, 1975) have been inconclusive as well. Abundant research has explored the effects of family violence on youth who kill (King, 1975; Miller & Looney, 1974; Podolsky, 1965). For example, King (1975) notes that the young killers in his sample had often been abused, and that the episodes of violence launched against them were an integral factor in their later homicidal behavior. Pfeffer (1980) reports similar findings.

Busch, Zagar, Hughes, Arbit, and Bussell (1990) compared a group of juveniles who killed with another group of nonviolent delinquents. The murder group contained 71 adjudicated youth (4 females and 67 males) between the ages of 10 and 17 (average age, 15.03). Busch et al. found that four background factors differentiated the juveniles in the murder group from the nonviolent delinquent group: (a) criminally violent family members,

(b) gang participation, (c) alcohol abuse, and (d) severe educational difficulties. Youth who killed came from backgrounds that included family members who were violent inside the family itself as well as members who were in jail and prison for violent offenses. These family members often included fathers, mothers, aunts, uncles, and grandparents "who committed homicide, assault, battery, rape, armed robbery, stabbing and shooting" (Busch et al., 1990, p. 484). Corder, Ball, and Hazlip (1976) and Hazlip, Corder, and Ball (1964) report that abusive parents, chronic alcoholism on the part of the parents, incarcerations for criminal activities, and repeated hospitalizations for psychosis are elements found in the backgrounds of youthful homicidal offenders. The researchers cited above also note that often children who kill are involved in gang activities, especially in urban areas.

Lewis et al. (1985) studied 24 incarcerated juveniles who had been committed to a clinical setting, but not for violent acts. Their results yield a picture of future killers who displayed a constellation of biopsychosocial characteristics, including psychotic symptoms, major neurological impairment, having a psychotic first-degree relative, violent acts during childhood, and severe physical abuse. According to these researchers, a combination of these components may account for those who have already killed and those who continue to do so.

Despite a great deal of research, there does not appear to be any one clear indicator, or set of indicators, capable of identifying which children are likely to kill. Many different elements seem to be involved in the development of the juvenile homicide offender—including social, biological, and family functioning factors—and we are unable to pinpoint precise combinations of these factors that will with some certainty result in a young person with a propensity to kill.

In Utah, Dr. Al Carlisle, a prison psychologist, is currently involved in psychological sessions with juveniles who murder (personal communication, March 28, 1991). Carlisle is finding that his research is confirming many earlier studies' findings regarding the backgrounds of the children who exercise fatal violence. His sample includes children with histories of life-threatening illness in early childhood, children from families in which physical and sexual violence are commonplace, and children who have attended schools where violence is a part of the atmosphere. In addition, he has noted that many of the children in his sample have histories of drug and alcohol abuse as well as gang involvement.

However, Carlisle believes he has discovered another dimension to the etiology of children who kill: a fantasy life that is distinct and unique to these types of children. He asserts that there is a relationship between the degree to which a person dissociates him- or herself from reality and fatal violence. Dissociation may come in the relatively mild form of daydreaming, which is especially prevalent among children in classroom situations, or it may be a complete detachment from reality. Carlisle notes that daydreaming is, of course, more prevalent than psychotic reactions in the young people he is studying, based on levels of dissociation he has measured through the use of psychometric scales. Carlisle believes that a child who breaks from reality may be more prone to exercise fatal violence. For example, children who fantasize more than others tend also to be more sensitive. For these children reality may become a threat, and to escape this threat they retreat to a fantasy world, where they feel no pain or hurt. Violence can be one method of dealing with a threat, real or imagined.

Carlisle's observations concerning dissociation and the role of fantasy or daydreaming in children who kill have not yet been validated by empirical research. However, this theory has some interesting parallels in the first author's own experience with and research on serial killers. He has often noted not only the role of fantasy in the launching phase of their murders, but the fact that the murderers have experienced some dissociation during their acts and tend to refer to some disconnected parts of themselves as the instigators of their crimes. Ted Bundy called this his "1% taking over," another serialist called it "my beast," and yet another termed it "the shadow." Research in this area needs to be continued.

TREATMENT OF
VIOLENT JUVENILE OFFENDERS

Little progress has been made not only in the understanding of the violent juvenile offender but also in the treatment of such youth. One impediment to treatment is that often the child is almost an adult when he or she comes before the criminal justice system. This is true not only in the United States but in other countries as well. For example, Rydelius (1988) reports that in Sweden, in a 10-year period, the average age of the youth who appeared before the court was 16 (there is no mention of when the acts themselves occurred).

One strategy that might aid in the reduction of juvenile homicide is early intervention. It is important that we identify not only the personal and social traits of children who kill, but also strategies to deal with the problem effectively once these children have been identified.

One treatment strategy that has been used with some success is the therapeutic wilderness camp-type program. In such programs, usually for adolescents ages 12-17, the youth attend therapeutic sessions, including individual and group counseling, take part in group "trust adventures," and participate in other activities designed to build self-esteem, trust, and so on.

At the MacLaren School for Boys in Oregon, many youths who have committed violent acts, including murder, are involved in a secure intensive treatment program. The "students" are placed in the program by an administrative decision of the staff at the institution. After a period of orientation that lasts at least five days, the student begins the program, which relies heavily on group confrontation and individual attention to enhance the student's self-awareness, communication skills, stress and anger management, values clarification, conflict resolution, and general interpersonal skills. Each student is encouraged to examine himself and his behaviors introspectively. The youth must "take ownership of his own problems" and make a written plan for his future.

In one group session we observed, eight youths participated. One 16-year-old was incarcerated for the murder of several elderly women. Another had been sent to MacLaren for the murder of his brother, and another had been incarcerated for repeated acts of violence, including rape and assault. Each student was forced to listen to the reactions of the others to his behavior during the day. The session was tense and tough; it was no place for the faint of heart. One youth had to be forcibly removed from the group session and placed in solitary confinement. The group manager and his assistant were aided by a former rapist who had only recently been granted parole from the Oregon State Penitentiary. He was included because he was so familiar with the "games played" by offenders—after all, he had played these games for years, not only on the streets but in the 20 years he had spent in prison.

The exact success rates of programs such as the ones described here are unknown. They vary according to the definition of *success* and depend on such factors as time, offense measured, and control of intake. These treatment programs appear to be a promising beginning, however.

CONCLUSION

The motivations of young people who kill are clearly deserving of closer examination. As noted throughout this chapter, research is being done in this area; obviously, we do not yet know enough about what leads children to become killers.

In the personal research of the first author, in dealing with serial murderers, all adults, several have mentioned that they either committed murder as youths or had strong fantasies about fatally injuring someone. Left unnoticed and untreated, each, without exception, murdered without remorse and then murdered again.

It has been said that children are our most prized possession. If we as a society truly believe that this is so, then we should be directing greater effort, resources, and study toward gaining some understanding of children who kill.

NOTE

1. The South, as defined by Goetting (1989) for purposes of this study, included Delaware, Maryland, the District of Columbia, Virginia, West Virginia, North Carolina, South Carolina, Georgia, Florida, Kentucky, Tennessee, Alabama, Mississippi, Arkansas, Louisiana, Oklahoma, and Texas.

References

Abel, G., Becker, J., Murphy, W., & Flanagan, B. (1981). Identifying dangerous child molesters. In R. B. Stuart (Ed.), *Violent behavior: Social learning approaches to prediction, management and treatment*. New York: Brunner/Mazel.

Abel, G., Mittelman, M., Becker, J., Rathner, J., & Rouleau, J. (1988). Predicting child molesters' response to treatment. In R. A. Prentky & V. L. Quinsey (Eds.), *Human sexual aggression: Current perspectives*. New York: New York Academy of Sciences.

American Psychiatric Association. (1987). *Diagnostic and statistical manual of mental disorders* (3rd ed., rev.). Washington, DC: Author.

Anti-Defamation League of B'nai B'rith, Civil Rights Division. (1983). *The "identity churches": A theology of hate*. New York.

Anti-Defamation League of B'nai B'rith, Civil Rights Division. (1987a). *The Committee of the States*. New York.

Anti-Defamation League of B'nai B'rith, Civil Rights Division. (1987b). *The hate movement today: A chronicle of violence and disarray*. New York.

Anti-Defamation League of B'nai B'rith, Civil Rights Division. (1987c). *The Pace Amendment*. New York.

Anti-Defamation League of B'nai B'rith, Civil Rights Division. (1988). *Hate groups in America*. New York.

Anti-Defamation League of B'nai B'rith, Civil Rights Division. (1989). *Extremism targets the prisons*. New York.

Baker, M., & Brompton, S. (1974). *Exclusive! The inside story of Patricia Hearst and the SLA*. New York: Macmillan.

Barnard, G. W., Vera, H., Vera, M., & Newman, G. (1982). Till death do us part: A study of spouse murder. *Bulletin of the American Academy of Psychiatry and Law, 10,* 271-280.

Barry, R. (1984). Incest: The last taboo (Part 1). *FBI Law Enforcement Bulletin, 53*(1), 2-9.

Bartholomew, A., Milte, K., & Galbally, F. (1978). Homosexual necrophilia. *Medicine, Science and the Law, 18,* 29-35.

Bartol, C. (1991). *Criminal behavior: A psychosocial approach.* Englewood Cliffs, NJ: Prentice-Hall.

Bartol, C., with Bartol, A. (1986). *Criminal behavior: A psychosocial approach.* Englewood Cliffs, NJ: Prentice-Hall.

Bernard, F. (1975). An inquiry among a group of pedophiles. *Journal of Sex Research, 11,* 242-255.

Bernick, B., & Spangler, J. (1985, September). Rovers kill up to 5,000 each year, experts say. *Desert News* (Las Vegas), p. A5.

Blackburn, D. (1990). *Human harvest: The Sacramento murder case.* New York: Knightsbridge.

Bolton, F., Morris, L., & MacEachron, A. (1989). *Males at risk: The other side of child sexual abuse.* Newbury Park, CA: Sage.

Bolz, F. (1980). *Hostage cop.* New York: Rawson, Wade.

Bolz, F. (1984, May). *Hostage negotiation training.* Workshop presented to the Grand Rapids Police Department, Grand Rapids, MI.

Bourget, D., & Bradford, J. (1987). Fire fetishism, diagnostic and clinical implications: A review of two cases. *Canadian Journal of Psychiatry, 32,* 459-462.

Brickman, A., McManus, M., Grapentine, W., & Alessi, N. (1984). Neuropsychological assessment of seriously delinquent adolescents. *Journal of the American Academy of Child and Adolescent Psychiatry, 23,* 453-467.

Brill, A. (1941). Necrophilia. *Journal of Criminal Psychopathology, 2,* 51-73.

Broder, B., Dunivant, N., & Smith, E. (1981). Further observation on the link between learning disability and juvenile delinquency. *Journal of Education Psychology, 43,* 838-850.

Brody, J. E. (1981). Researchers trace key factors in profiles of assassins on the American scene. *New York Times,* p. A1.

Brown, R. (1979). Historical patterns of American violence. In H. Graham & T. R. Gurr (Eds.), *Violence in America: Historical and comparative perspectives,* Beverly Hills, CA: Sage.

Brown, S., Esbensen, F., & Geis, G. (1991). *Criminology: Explaining crime and its context.* Cincinnati, OH: Anderson.

Browne, A. (1986). Assault and homicide: When battered women kill. *Advances in Applied Social Psychology, 3,* 57-79.

Browne, A. (1987). *When battered women kill.* New York: Free Press.

Browne, A., & Williams, K. R. (1987, November 11-14). *Resource availability for women at risk: Its relationship to rates of female-perpetrated partner homicide.* Paper presented at the annual meeting of the American Society of Criminology, Montreal.

Bugliosi, V. (1975). *Helter skelter: The true story of the Manson murders.* New York: W. W. Norton.

Bullard, S. (1991). *The Ku Klux Klan: A history of racism and violence.* Montgomery, AL: Klanwatch.

Burg, B. (1982). The sick and the dead: The development of psychological theory on necrophilia from Kraft-Ebbing to the present. *Journal of the History of Behavioral Sciences, 218,* 242-254.

Busch, K., Zagar, R., Hughes, J., Arbit, J., & Bussell, R. (1990). Adolescents who kill. *Journal of Clinical Psychology, 46,* 472-485.

192   *Murder in America*

Buzawa, E., & Buzawa, C. (1990). *Domestic violence: The criminal justice response.* Newbury Park, CA: Sage.

Calef, V., & Weinshel, E. (1972). On certain equivalents of necrophilia. *International Journal of Psychoanalysis, 42,* 67-75.

Came, B., & Bergman, B. (1990, October 22). Victims in the home: Domestic violence in Quebec. *Canada,* p. 18.

Caputo, P. (1989, December). Death goes to school. *Esquire,* pp. 137-155.

Carmody, D. C., & Williams, K. R. (1987). Wife assault and perceptions of sanctions. *Violence and Victims, 2*(1).

Chalmers, D. (1965). *Hooded Americanism: The first century of the Ku Klux Klan.* Garden City, NY: Doubleday.

Cleckley, H. (1982). *The mask of sanity.* New York: Plume.

Cohler, L. (1989). Republican racist: Dealing with the David Duke problem. *New Republic, 201,* 11-14.

Cohn, E., & Berk, L. (1987). *Police policy on domestic violence, 1986: A national survey.* Washington, DC: Crime Control Institute.

Conklin, J. E. (1989). *Criminology* (3rd ed.). New York: Macmillan.

Conway, Z. (1989). Factors predicting verdicts in cases where battered women kill their husbands. *Law and Human Behavior, 13,* 253-269.

Cooper, H. (1982). What is a terrorist? A psychological perspective. *Legal Medical Quarterly, 1,* 8-18.

Corcoran, J. (1991). *Bitter harvest: Gordon Kahl and the Posse Comitatus: Murder in the heartland.* New York: Penguin.

Corder, B., Ball, B., & Hazlip, T. (1976). Adolescent parricide: A comparison with other adolescent murder. *American Journal of Psychiatry, 133,* 957-961.

Crazy Pat's revenge. (1986, September 1). *Time,* p. 19.

Daly, M., & Wilson, M. (1988). *Homicide.* New York: Aldine de Gruyter.

Death on the playground. (1989, January 30). *Newsweek,* p. 35.

DeFrancis, V. (1969). *Protecting the child victim of sex crimes committed by parents.* Denver, CO: American Humane Society.

Dettlinger, C. (1983). *The list.* Atlanta, GA: Philmay.

Deykin, E., Levy, J., & Wells, V. (1987). Adolescent depression, alcohol and drug use. *American Journal of Public Health, 77,* 178-181.

Dietz, P. (1986). Mass, serial and sensational homicides. *Bulletin of the New York Academy of Medicine, 62,* 477-491.

D'Orban, P. (1990). Female homicide. *Irish Journal of Psychological Medicine, 7,* 64-70.

Duncan, J., & Duncan, G. (1971). Murder in the family; A study of some homicidal adolescents. *American Journal of Psychiatry, 127,* 1498-1502.

Eckert, A. (1985). *The scarlet mansion.* New York: Bantam.

Egger, S. (1990). *Serial murder: An elusive phenomenon.* New York: Praeger.

Elkind, P. (1989). *The death shift.* New York: Onyx.

Ellis, A. (1986). *The encyclopedia of sexual behavior.* New York: Hawthorne.

Ellis, H. (1946). *Psychology of sex: A manual for students.* New York: Jason Aronson.

Erlanger, H. (1976). Is there a subculture of violence in the South? *Journal of Criminal Law and Criminology, 66,* 483-490.

Ewing, C. (1987). *Battered women who kill.* Lexington, MA: Lexington.

Ewing, C. (1990). *When children kill: The dynamics of juvenile homicide.* Lexington, MA: Lexington.

Faguet, R. (1980). Munchausen syndrome and necrophilia. *Suicide and Life-Threatening Behavior, 10,* 214-218.

Farr, L. (1992). *The Sunset murders.* New York: Pocket Books.

Federal Bureau of Investigation. (1986). *Analysis of terrorist incidents in the United States.* Washington, DC: Government Printing Office.

Feld, L. S., & Straus, M. A. (1989). Escalation and desistance of wife assault in marriage. *Criminology, 27,* 141-161.

Fishbain, D., Rao, V., & Aldrich, T. (1985). Female homicide-suicide perpetrators: A controlled study. *Journal of Forensic Science, 30,* 1148-1156.

Freire, A. (1981). The necrophiliac character according to Erich Fromm: The case of Amanda. *Psiquis: Revista de Psiquiartria, Psicologia y Psciosomatica, 2,* 23-32.

Frisbie, L. (1965). Treated sex offenders who reverted to sexually deviant behavior. *Federal Probation, 29,* 52-57.

Gainey, T. (1989). *Innocent blood.* New York: St. Martin's.

Garner, J., & Clemmer, E. (1985). *Danger to police in domestic violence disturbances: A new look.* Washington, DC: U.S. Department of Justice, Office of Justice Programs.

Gastil, R. (1971). Homicide and the regional culture of violence. *American Sociological Review, 39,* 412-427.

Geberth, V. (1991). Lust murder: The psychodynamics of the killer and the psychosexual aspects of the crime. *Law and Order, 39*(6), 70-75.

Gelles, R. J. (1974). *The violent home: A study of physical aggression between husbands and wives.* Beverly Hills, CA: Sage.

Gelles, R. J. (1979). *Family violence.* Beverly Hills, CA: Sage.

Gelles, R. J., & Pedrick-Cornell, C. (Eds.). (1983). *International perspective on family violence.* Lexington, MA: Lexington.

Gelles, R. J., & Straus, M. A. (1985). Violence in the American family. In A. J. Lincoln & M. A. Straus (Eds.), *Crime in the family* (pp. 88-110). Springfield, IL: Charles C Thomas.

Gelles, R. J., & Straus, M. A. (1989). *Intimate violence: The causes and consequences of abuse in the American family.* New York: Simon & Schuster.

Gilbert, J. (1990). *Criminal investigation.* Toronto: Charles E. Merrill.

Gillies, H. (1976). Homicide in the west of Scotland. *British Journal of Psychology, 128,* 105-127.

Goetting, A. (1987). Homicidal wives: A profile. *Journal of Family Issues, 8,* 332-341.

Goetting, A. (1989). Patterns of marital homicide: A comparison of husbands and wives. *Journal of Comparative Family Studies, 2,* 341-354.

Goetting, A. (1993). Patterns of homicide among children. In A. Wilson (Ed.), *Homicide: The victim/offender connection.* Cincinnati, OH: Anderson.

Gollmar, R. (1982). *Edward Gein: America's most bizarre murderer.* Delavan, WI: Charles Hallberg.

Golman, D. (1986, September 4). The roots of terrorism are found in brutality of shattered childhood. *New York Times,* pp. C1, C8.

Goolkasian, G. A. (1986). *Confronting domestic violence: A guide for criminal justice agencies.* Washington, DC: U.S. Department of Justice, National Institute of Justice.

Gross, J. (1988, September 10). Calming the storm: Patty Hearst's new life. *New York Times,* pp. C1, C8.

Groth, A., Longo, R., & McFadin, J. (1990). Undetected recidivism among rapists and child molesters. In D. Kelly (Ed.), *Criminal behavior: Text and readings in criminology* (2nd ed.). New York: St. Martin's.

Gurr, T. R. (1988). Political terrorism in the United States: Historical antecedents and contemporary trends. In M. Stohl (Ed.), *The politics of terrorism* (3rd ed., rev., pp. 549-578). New York: Marcel Dekker.

Gutteridge, W. (1986). *Contemporary terrorism.* New York: Facts on File.

Hacker, F. (1976). *Crusaders, criminals, and crazies.* New York: W. W. Norton.

Hagaman, J., Wells,. G., & Blau, T. (1987). Psychological profile of family homicide. *Police Chief, 54,* 19-22.

Hamparian, D., Davis, J., Jacobson, J., & McGraw, R. (1985). *The young criminal years of the violent few.* Washington, DC: U.S. Department of Justice, Office of Juvenile Justice and Delinquency Prevention, National Institute of Juvenile Justice and Delinquency Prevention.

Hamparian, D., Schuster, D., Dinitz, S., & Conrad, J. (1978). *The violent few: A study of dangerous juvenile offenders.* Lexington, MA: D. C. Heath.

Hansen, M., & Harway, M. (Eds.). (1993). *Battering and family therapy: A feminist perspective.* Newbury Park, CA: Sage.

Harris, J. (1987). Domestic terrorism in the 1980s. *FBI Law Enforcement Bulletin, 56,* 5-13.

Hazelwood, R., & Douglas, J. (1980). The lust murder. *FBI Law Enforcement Bulletin, 49*(4), 1-8.

Hazlip, T., Corder, B., & Ball, B. (1964). The adolescent murderer. In C. Keith (Ed.), *The violent adolescent.* New York: Free Press.

Heide, K. (1993). Adolescent parricide offenders: Synthesis, illustration and future directions. In A. Wilson (Ed.), *Homicide: The victim/offender connection.* Cincinnati, OH: Anderson.

Herek, G., & Berrill, K. (1992). *Hate crimes: Confronting violence against lesbians and gay men.* Newbury Park, CA: Sage.

Hickey, E. (1991). *Serial killers and their victims.* Pacific Grove, CA: Brooks/ Cole.

Hoffman, B. (1987). Terrorism in the United States in 1985. In P. Wilkinson & A. Stewart (Eds.), *Contemporary research on terrorism.* Aberdeen, Scotland: Aberdeen University Press.

Holmes, R. M. (1983). *The sex offender and the criminal justice system.* Springfield, IL: Charles C Thomas.

Holmes, R. M. (1989). *Profiling violent crimes: An investigative tool.* Newbury Park, CA: Sage.

Holmes, R. M. (1990). Human hunters: A new type of serial killer. *Knightbeat, 9*(1), 43-47.

Holmes, R. M. (1991). *Sex crimes.* Newbury Park, CA: Sage.

Holmes, R. M., & De Burger, J. (1985). Profiles in terror: The serial murderer. *Federal Probation, 53,* 53-59.

Holmes, R. M., & De Burger, J. (1988). *Serial murder.* Newbury Park, CA: Sage.
Holmes, R. M., De Burger, J., & Holmes, S. T. (1990). Inside the mind of the serial murderer. *American Journal of Criminal Justice, 13,* 1-9.
Holmes, R. M., & Holmes, S. T. (1992). Understanding mass murder: A starting point. *Federal Probation, 56,* 53-61.
Home Box Office. (1988). *Murder: No apparent motive.*
Homer, F. D. (1983). Terror in the United States: Three perspectives. In M. Stone (Ed.), *The politics of terrorism.* New York: Marcel Dekker.
Howard, M. (1986). Husband-wife homicide: An essay from a family law perspective. *Law and Contemporary Problems, 49,* 63-88.
Humphrey, J., & Palmer, S. (1987). Stressful life events and criminal homicide. *Omega, 17,* 299-306.
Jamieson, K., & Flanagan, T. (1988). *Sourcebook of criminal justice statistics, 1988.* Washington, DC: U.S. Department of Justice, Bureau of Justice Statistics.
Jenkins, P. (1988). Serial murder in England 1940-1985. *Journal of Criminal Justice, 16,* 1-15.
Kalichman, S. (1988). MMPI profiles of women and men convicted of domestic homicide. *Journal of Clinical Psychology, 44,* 847-853.
Katchadourian, H., & Lunde, D. (1975). *Fundamentals of human sexuality.* New York: Holt, Rinehart & Winston.
Kerstetter, W. A. (1983). Terrorism. In S. H. Kadish (Ed.), *Encyclopedia of crime and justice.* New York: Free Press.
King, C. (1975). The ego and the integration of violence in homicidal youth. *American Journal of Orthopsychiatry, 45,* 134-145.
Kirkham, J., Levy, S., & Crofty, W. (1970). *Assassinations and political violence* (Staff report to the National Commission on the Causes and Prevention of Violence). Washington, DC: Government Printing Office.
Knox, D. (1984). *Human sexuality: The search for understanding.* St. Paul, MN: West.
Korbin, J. (1986). Childhood histories of women imprisoned for fatal child maltreatment. *Child Abuse and Neglect, 10,* 331-338.
Kratcoski, P. (1987). Families who kill. *Marriage and Family Review, 12,* 47-70.
Lancaster, N. (1978). Necrophilia, murder and high intelligence: A case report. *British Journal of Psychiatry, 132,* 605-608.
Langan, P., & Innes, C. (1986). *Preventing domestic violence against women* (Bureau of Justice Statistics Special Report). Washington, DC: U.S. Department of Justice, Office of Justice Programs.
Langlois, J. (1985). *Belle Gunness.* Bloomington: Indiana University Press.
Laqueur, W. (1988). *The age of terrorism.* Boston: Little, Brown.
LaVey, A. (1969). *The Satanic bible.* New York: Dell.
Leavitt, P. (1991, July 25). Operation Rescue founder jailed. *USA Today,* p. 3A.
Lerman, L. (1981). *Prosecution of spouse abuse: Innovations in criminal justice response.* Washington, DC: Center for Women's Policy Studies.
Lester, D. (1987). Benefits of marriage for reducing risk of violent death. *Psychological Reports, 61,* p. 198.
Levin, J., & Fox, J. (1985). *Mass murder.* New York: Plenum.
Lewis, D., & Shanok, S. (1977). Medical histories of psychiatrically referred delinquent children. *American Journal of Psychiatry, 134,* 491-432.

Lewis, D., Shanok, S., Grant, M., & Ritvo, E. (1983). Homicidally aggressive young children: Neuropsychiatric and experimental correlates. *American Journal of Psychiatry, 140,* 148-153.

Lewis, D., Moy, E., Jackson, L., Aronson, R., Restifo, S., & Simos, A. (1985). Biopsychosocial characteristics of children who later murder: A prospective study. *American Journal of Psychiatry, 142,* 1161-1167.

Lewis, D., Pincus, J., Bard, B. Richardson, E., Prichep, L., Feldman, M., & Yeager, C. (1988). Neuropsychiatric, psychoeducational and family characteristics of 14 juveniles condemned to death in the United States. *American Journal of Psychiatry, 146,* 1243-1269.

Lewis, S., & Grant, R. (1983). Homicidally aggressive young children: Neuropsychiatric and experiential correlates. *American Journal of Psychiatry, 148.*

Lieberman, M. (1991). The Hate Crimes Statistics Act. *Journal, 20*(2), 9-12.

Lilly, J., Cullen, F., & R. Ball. (1989). *Criminological theory: Context and consequences.* Newbury Park, CA: Sage.

Linedecker, C., & Burt, W. (1990). *Nurses who kill.* New York: Windsor.

Livesey, C. (1980). *The Manson women.* New York: Richard Marek.

Lofton, C., & Hill, R. (1974). Regional subculture of violence: An examination of the Gastil-Hackney thesis. *American Sociological Review, 39,* 714-724.

Lowenstein, L. (1989). Homicide: A review of recent research (1975-1985). *Criminologist, 13*(2), 74-89.

Lunde, D. (1977). *Murder and madness.* San Francisco: San Francisco.

Magnuson, E. (1989, March 6). An ex-Klansman's win brings the chickens home to roost. *Time,* p. 29.

Mann, C. (1988). Getting even? Women who kill in domestic encounters. *Justice Quarterly, 5,* 33-51.

Marshall, B., & Williams, P. (1991). *Zero to the bone.* New York: Pocket Star.

Marshall, W., & Barbaree, H. (1988). An outpatient treatment program for child molesters. In R. A. Prentky & V. L. Quinsey (Eds.), *Human sexual aggression: Current perspectives.* New York: New York Academy of Sciences.

Marshall, W., & Christie, M. (1981). Pedophiles and aggression. *Criminal Justice & Behavior, 8,* 145-158.

Masters, R., & Robertson, C. (1990). *Inside criminology.* Englewood Cliffs, NJ: Prentice-Hall.

McGuire, C., & Norton, C. (1988). *Perfect victim.* New York: Dell.

McKnight, C., Mohr, J., & Quinsey, R. (1966). Mental illness and homicide. *Canadian Psychiatric Association Journal, 11,* 91-98.

The men who murdered. (1985). *FBI Law Enforcement Bulletin, 54*(8), 2-6.

Mercy, J., & Saltzman, L. (1989). Fatal violence among spouses in the United States. *American Journal of Public Health, 79,* 595-599.

Merkl, P. (1986). *Political violence and terror: Motifs and motivations.* Berkeley: University of California Press.

Messner, S., & Tardiff, H. (1985). The social ecology of urban homicide: An application of the "routine activities" approach. *Criminology, 23,* 241-267.

Michaud, S., & Aynesworth, H. (1983). *The only living witness.* New York: Signet.

Mickolus, E., Sandler, T., & Murdock, J. (1989). *International terrorism in the 1980s.* Ames: Iowa State University Press.

Miller, D., & Looney, J. (1974). The prediction of adolescent homicide: Episodic dyscontrol and dehumanization. *American Journal of Psychoanalysis, 34,* 187-198.

Mohr, J., Turner, R., & Jerry, M. (1964). *Pedophiles and exhibitionism.* Toronto: University of Toronto Press.

Money, J. (1984). Paraphilias: Phenomenology and classification. *American Journal of Psychotherapy, 38,* 164-179.

Nash, J. (1980). *Murder, America: Homicide in the United States from the revolution to the present.* New York: Evans.

Nettler, G. (1982). *Killing one another.* Cincinnati, OH: Anderson.

New York Task Force on Women in the Courts. (1984). Report of the New York Task Force on Women in the Courts. *Fordham Urban Law Journal, 15,* 11, 198.

Nice, D. C. (1988). Abortion clinic bombings as political violence. *American Journal of Political Science, 32,* 178-195.

Noguchi, T. (1985). *Coroner at large.* New York: Pocket Books.

Norris, J. (1988). *Serial killers: The growing menace.* New York: Dolphin.

Norris, J. (1991). *Henry Lee Lucas: The shocking true story of America's most notorious serial killer.* New York: Kensington.

Parry, A. (1976). *Terrorism.* New York: Vanguard.

Pfeffer, C. (1980). Psychiatric hospital treatment of assaultive homicidal children. *American Journal of Psychotherapy, 34,* 197-207.

Podolsky, E. (1964). The chemistry of murder. *Pakistan Medical Journal, 15,* 9-14.

Podolsky, E. (1965). Children who kill. *General Practice, 31*(5), 98-102.

Poinsett, A. (1987, December). Why are our children killing one another? *Ebony,* pp. 88-90.

Police Foundation. (1976). *Domestic violence and the police: Studies in Detroit and Kansas City.* Washington, DC: Author.

Pontius, A. (1982). Neurological aspects of some types of delinquency, especially in juveniles. *Adolescence, 7,* 289-308.

Post, G. (1987). Rewarding fire with fire: Effects of retaliation on terrorist army dynamics. *Terrorism, 10,* 23-36.

Rapoport, D. (1988). *Inside terrorist organizations.* New York: Columbia University Press.

Reinhardt, J. (1973). The dismal tunnel: Depression before murder. *International Journal of Offender Therapy and Comparative Criminology, 13,* 246-249.

Ressler, R., Burgess, A., & Douglas, J. (1988). *Sexual homicide: Patterns, motives and procedures for investigation.* New York: Free Press.

Revitch, E., & Weiss, R. (1962). The pedophilic offender. *Diseases of the Nervous System, 23,* 73-78.

Reynolds, B. (1990, August 30). This is the beginning of the end for murderer. *USA Today.*

Righton, P. (1981). The adult. In B. Taylor (Ed.), *Perspectives on paedophilia* (pp. 16-19). London: Batsford Academic and Educational.

Rosman, J., & Resnick, P. (1989). Sexual attraction to corpses: A psychiatric review of necrophilia. *Bulletin of the American Academy of Psychiatry and the Law, 17,* 153-163.

Rowley, J., Ewing, C., & Singer, S. (1987). Juvenile homicide: The need for an interdisciplinary approach. *Behavioral Sciences and the Law, 5,* 1-10.

Rule, A. (1983). *The stranger beside me.* New York: Signet.

Rule, A. (1988). *The I-5 killer.* New York: Signet.

Rush, G. (1991). *The dictionary of criminal justice* (3rd ed.). Guilford, CT: Dushkin.

Rydelius, P. (1988). The development of antisocial behavior and sudden violent death. *Acta Psychiatrica Scandinavica, 77,* 398-403.

Satterfield, J., Hoppe, C., & Schell, A. (1982). A prospective study of delinquency in 110 adolescent boys with attention deficit disorder and 88 normal boys. *American Journal of Psychiatry, 139,* 395-427.

Scanlon, L., & Wolfson, A. (1989, September 15). Disturbed worker kills 7 and wounds 13 in rampage with AK-47 at Louisville plant. *Courier-Journal* (Louisville, KY).

Schechter, H. (1990). *Deranged.* New York: Pocket Books.

Schiller, L. (1970). *The killing of Sharon Tate.* New York: New American Library.

Schmid, A. P., & De Graaf, J. (1982). *Violence as communication: Insurgent terrorism and the Western news media.* Beverly Hills, CA: Sage.

Schreiber, F. (1984). *The Shoemaker: The anatomy of a psychotic.* New York: Signet.

Schultz, R. (1975). *Rape victimology.* Springfield, IL: Charles C Thomas.

Sendi, I., & Blomgren, P. (1975). A comparative study of predictive criteria in the predisposition of homicidal adolescents. *American Journal of Psychiatry, 132,* 423-427.

Sherman, L. W., & Berk, R. A. (1984). The specific deterrent effect of arrest for domestic assault. *American Sociological Review, 49,* 261-272.

Simpson, J. (1989, January 9). Beware of paper tigers. *Time,* pp. 104-105.

Slaughter in a school yard. (1989, January 30). *Time,* p. 29.

Smith, C., & Gullen, T. (1991). *The search for the Green River Killer.* New York: Penguin.

Smith, P. (1989). Perfect murders. *New Statesman and Society, 57*(2), 1-9.

Soler, E. (1987). Domestic violence is a crime: A case study of the San Francisco family violence project. In D. J. Sonkin (Ed.), *Domestic violence on trial: Psychological and legal dimensions of family violence.* New York: Springer.

Squiteri, T. (1991). Murder "tide" is still rising. *USA Today,* p. 1A.

Stack, A. (1983). *The lust killer.* New York: Signet.

State v. Thorton, Tenn., 730 S.W.2d 309 (1987).

Statten, J., Menninger, K., & Rosen, I. (1960). Murder with apparent motive: A study in personality disorganization. *American Journal of Psychiatry, 117,* 48-53.

Sterling, C. (1981). *The terror network.* New York: Holt, Rinehart & Winston.

Stermac, L., Hall, K., & Henskens, M. (1989). Violence among child molesters. *Journal of Sex Research, 20,* 450-459.

Stinson, J. (1984, November). *Assessing terrorist tactics and security measures.* Paper presented at the Detroit Police Department conference, "Urban Terrorism: Planning or Chaos?"

Stohl, M. (Ed.). (1988). *The politics of terrorism* (3rd ed., rev.). New York: Marcel Dekker.

Stordeur, R. A., & Stille, R. (1989). *Ending men's violence against their partners: One road to peace.* Newbury Park, CA: Sage.

Straus, M. A., & Gelles, R. J. (1986). Societal change and change in family violence from 1975 to 1985 as revealed by two national surveys. *Journal of Marriage and the Family, 48,* 465-479.

Straus, M. A., Gelles, R. J., & Steinmetz, S. K. (1980). *Behind closed doors: Violence in the American family.* Garden City, NY: Anchor/Doubleday.

Strentz, T. (1988). A terrorist's psychosocial profile, past and present. *FBI Law Enforcement Bulletin, 57,* 13-19.

Sullivan, T., & Maiken, P. (1983). *The killer clown.* New York: Grosset & Dunlap.

10 minutes of madness. (1986, September 1). *Newsweek,* p. 18.

Toupinm, J. (1993). Adolescent murderers: Validation of a typology and study of their recidivism. In A. Wilson (Ed.), *Homicide: The victim/offender connection.* Cincinnati, OH: Anderson.

U.S. Attorney General's Task Force on Family Violence. (1984, September). *Final report.* Washington, DC: Government Printing Office.

U.S. Commission on Civil Rights. (1982). *Under the rule of thumb: Battered women and the administration of justice.* Washington, DC: Government Printing Office.

U.S. Department of Justice. (1988). *Terrorist group profiles.* Washington, DC: Government Printing Office.

U.S. Department of Justice, Bureau of Justice Statistics. (1989). *Report to the nation on crime and justice* (2nd ed.). Washington, DC: Government Printing Office.

U.S. Department of Justice, Bureau of Justice Statistics. (1991a). *Criminal victimization in the United States.* Washington, DC: Author.

U.S. Department of Justice, Bureau of Justice Statistics. (1991b). *Sourcebook of criminal justice statistics, 1991.* Washington, DC: Author.

U.S. Department of Justice, Federal Bureau of Investigation. (1980-1986). *Uniform crime reports for the United States: Crime in the United States.* Washington, DC: Government Printing Office.

U.S. Department of Justice, U.S. Marshals Service. (1989). *Skinheads.* Washington, DC: Government Printing Office.

U.S. Senate Judiciary Committee. (1991). *Report of the U.S. Senate Judiciary Committee.* Washington, DC: Government Printing Office.

van Hoffman, E. (1990). *A venom in the blood.* New York: Donald I. Fine.

Vetter, H., & Perlstein, G. (1991). *Perspectives on terrorism.* Belmont, CA: Brooks/Cole.

Vice President's Task Force. (1986). *Report of the Vice President's Task Force on Combating Terrorism.* Washington, DC: Government Printing Office.

Virkunnen, L. (1981). The child as participating victim. In M. Cook (Ed.), *Adult sexual interest in children.* London: Academic Press.

Vito, G., & Holmes, R. (1993). *Criminology: Research, policy and issues.* Belmont, CA: Wadsworth.

Walker, L. E. A. (1979). *The battered woman.* New York: Harper & Row.

Walker, L. E. A. (1983). The battered woman syndrome study. In D. Finkelhor, R. J. Gelles, G. T. Hotaling, & M. A. Straus (Eds.), *The dark side of families: Current family violence research.* Beverly Hills, CA: Sage.

Walker, L. E. A. (1984). *The battered woman syndrome*. New York: Springer.

Walker, L. E. A. (1989). *Terrifying love: Why battered women kill and how society responds*. New York: HarperCollins.

Walker, L. E. A. (1993). Legal self-defense for battered women. In M. Hansen & M. Harway (Eds.), *Battering and family therapy: A feminist perspective*. Newbury Park, CA: Sage.

Wedge, T. (1988). *The Satan hunter*. Canton, OH: Daring.

Weed, S., & Swanton, S. (1976). *My search for Patty Hearst*. New York: Crown.

Weeks, J. (1986). *Sexuality*. New York: Ellis Horowitz.

Weinberg, L., & Davis, P. (1989). *Introduction to political terrorism*. Englewood Cliffs, NJ: Prentice-Hall.

Weiner, N., Zahn, M., & Sagi, R. (1990). *Violence: Patterns, causes and public policy*. New York: Harcourt Brace Jovanovich.

White, J. (1991). *Terrorism: An introduction*. Belmont, CA: Brooks/Cole.

Whitehead, J., & Lab, S. (1989). *Juvenile justice: An introduction*. Cincinnati, OH: Anderson.

Wilbanks, W. (1983). The female offender in Dade County, Florida. *Criminal Justice Review, 8*(2).

Wilson, C., & Oden, R. (1987). *Jack the Ripper: Summing up and the verdict*. New York: Bantam.

Wolfe, D. (1985). Child-abusive parents: An empirical review and analysis. *Psychological Bulletin, 97,* 462-592.

Wolfgang, M., & Ferracuti, F. (1967). *The subculture of violence: Towards an integrated theory in criminology*. New York: Methuen.

Wong, M., & Singer, K. (1973). Abnormal homicide in Hong Kong. *Psychiatry, 123,* 295-298.

Index

About the Authors

Ronald M. Holmes is a Professor of Justice Administration at the University of Louisville, Department of Justice Administration. Dr. Holmes has lectured throughout the United States on sex crimes and homicide investigation. He has also assisted in more than 300 homicide cases for police departments. Dr. Holmes has published in scholarly journals and law enforcement publications on topics such as serial murder, sex crimes, and psychological profiling. He is the author of *Serial Murder, Profiling Violent Crimes, Sex Crimes,* and *The Sex Offender and the Criminal Justice System.*

Stephen T. Holmes is a doctoral student at the University of Cincinnati. He has also published in journals such as the *American Journal of Criminal Justice* and the *Contemporary Journal of Criminal Justice.* Holmes has researched in the areas of female homicide and serial murder as well as in other topics such as drug abuse and parole issues. He is scheduled to receive his doctoral degree in criminal justice in 1994.